# Principal Bootcamp

This book shows principals how they can accelerate their impact and make a difference from day one. Speaker and author Dr. Brad Johnson offers new and experienced principals authoritative advice on how to succeed in key areas: understanding the best leadership traits; developing positive relationships with staff; building a dynamic team culture; and creating a unified vision. Each chapter includes inspiring stories and practical examples for leaders in all types of school districts. Using these strategies, you will learn how to immediately maximize your influence over yourself, your staff, and the entire school culture.

**Dr. Brad Johnson** has over 20 years of experience as a teacher and administrator at the K–12 and collegiate level. He is a national speaker and author and is also on the national faculty for Concordia University School of Graduate Studies in Leadership. His other books include *Learning On Your Feet, From School Administrator to School Leader*, and *Putting Teachers First*.

T0386581

## Also Available from Routledge Eye On Education
(www.routledge.com/k-12)

Putting Teachers First: How to Inspire, Motivate, and Connect with Your Staff
Brad Johnson

Learning on Your Feet: Incorporating Physical Activity into the K-8 Classroom
Brad Johnson and Melody Jones

From School Administrator to School Leader: 15 Keys to Maximizing Your Leadership Potential
Brad Johnson and Julie Sessions

What Schools Don't Teach: 20 Ways to Help Students Excel in School and Life
Brad Johnson and Julie Sessions

What Great Teachers Do Differently, Third Edition: Nineteen Things That Matter Most
Todd Whitaker

What Great Principals Do Differently, Third Edition: Twenty Things That Matter Most
Todd Whitaker

# Principal Bootcamp

## Accelerated Strategies to Influence and Lead from Day One

Brad Johnson

Routledge
Taylor & Francis Group

NEW YORK AND LONDON

First published 2021
by Routledge
52 Vanderbilt Avenue, New York, NY 10017

and by Routledge
2 Park Square, Milton Park, Abingdon, Oxon, OX14 4RN

*Routledge is an imprint of the Taylor & Francis Group, an informa business*

© 2021 Taylor & Francis

*Library of Congress Cataloging-in-Publication Data*
A catalog record for this title has been requested

ISBN: 978-0-367-43310-9 (hbk)
ISBN: 978-0-367-43309-3 (pbk)
ISBN: 978-1-003-00240-6 (ebk)

Typeset in Palatino
by River Editorial Ltd, Devon, UK

# Contents

# Acknowledgements

I want to thank Lauren Davis for all her hard work, encouragement, and support over the past few years. She has been so helpful in helping me develop as an author and appreciate all she has done for me.

# Meet the Author

**Dr. Brad Johnson** is one of the most dynamic and engaging speakers in the fields of education and leadership. He has 25 years' experience in "The Trenches" as a teacher and administrator. He currently teaches graduate level classes in leadership.

Brad is transforming how teachers lead in the classroom and how administrators lead in the school. He is a selfless leader who shares his vast experiences and expertise to help other educators maximize their potential.

Brad is author of eight books including *Putting Teachers First: How to Inspire, Motivate, and Connect with Your Staff*, *Learning on Your Feet: Incorporating Physical Activity into the K-8 Classroom*, and *From School Administrator to School Leader: 15 Keys to Maximizing Your Leadership Potential*.

Brad has traveled the globe speaking and training teachers and educational leaders. One of his most memorable experiences was traveling throughout Malaysia speaking at teacher training centers.

# Introduction

Leadership has been a life's work of mine. I have served as an administrator, taught leadership courses in graduate school, mentored leaders, and interviewed elite leaders from various fields around the world. Through my own education, experiences, and experiences of others, I have come to the realization that leadership at its foundation is all about influence. How we influence our own self, influence others, and how we influence culture.

I chose a bootcamp theme because it is a military term that means to prepare recruits for service by providing them the training they need in a short amount of time. It gives them the tools, in an accelerated environment, necessary to perform the roles that will be assigned to them for the duration of their service. The very origin of leadership was founded by military disciplines and have resonated throughout all other areas of life, including education.

The term bootcamp is used in today's culture to describe everything from a specific type of fitness program to a leadership program. The business world is especially known for leadership bootcamps, where participants are immersed into a workshop to learn basic leadership skills in a short amount of time. The purpose of these bootcamps are to maximize success through inspiring, empowering, and challenging participants to build leadership skills in order to positively influence and contribute to organizational cultures.

Therefore, the goal of this book is to provide principals and other administrators the basic skills/tools necessary to perform their roles effectively. After all, I think **leadership should be seen as a privilege**, a privilege to serve, to serve the amazing team of people in your charge. As a principal or educational leader, you lead one of the most amazing group of professionals in the world, teachers and supporting staff!

I have compiled the key areas of influence that I have used over the past 25-plus years to help you maximize your potential in the shortest amount of time, so that you and your team experience much success. These include understanding best leadership traits, developing strong positive relationships with staff, building a dynamic team culture, and becoming a leader of influence.

This doesn't mean that I am the drill sergeant trying to tell you what to do, but think of me more as a guide sharing my experiences and the experiences of many other servant leaders, while helping you identify and build upon your own leadership strengths to be the best leader possible for your staff.

What makes the bootcamp concept so necessary for principals, is the high turnover rate. The turnover rate for principals is three to five years. This means principals are given very little time to influence the school culture. Gone are the days when they were basically hired for as long as they desired to serve. Now they are under immense pressure to raise test scores, create better school cultures, or fix some other problem. When administrators are put under this type of pressure, **they often focus too much on the problems for which they were hired than to focus on the staff, which is often the solution to helping them with the problems**.

Even when there are no problems, there are districts that feel like they need to switch things and keep principals moving. This means principals no longer have years to get buy in from teachers and to build strong relationships. It needs to be done as quickly as possible and that is again where this book comes in. These chapters will focus on the strategies needed to maximize your influence over self, your staff, as well as the school culture immediately. So, are you ready to report for duty and lead from day one?

# 1

# Influencing Yourself

## The Call to Duty

If you ask most teachers why they got into teaching, most will share the story of a teacher or teachers who profoundly influenced them. I have had several amazing teachers throughout the years who greatly influenced me. But the person who had the greatest influence on me was actually my high school principal, Mr. Kent. He had already been the principal for years before I attended the high school, so he already had time to build a strong school culture with staff, parents, and community and trust me it showed! What I remember most was how calm and laid-back he was as principal of the school.

He would greet students and teachers as they entered the school each morning. He would take time to talk and listen in the hallways and the cafeteria. He would stop into classes just to see what was going on without a teacher evaluation in sight. Not that I would have recognized a teacher evaluation form, but he usually just had the two-way radio (yes, this was before cell phones) in his hand. He seemed to know every student, every parent, and connected with his teachers in a very caring way. He never seemed to be too stressed, even though I know some of the students, parents, and yes probably some teachers caused him to turn gray prematurely.

But what I remember most happened when I scored in the 99th percentile in every subject of the high stakes testing we took back then. Yes, we had them back then too! Besides a certificate and award for the accomplishment, he actually used his own money to purchase a watch for me. Now on a principal's salary, it was not a Rolex, but I treasured that watch for many years as if it were a Rolex. It showed that he really cared and he was one to celebrate successes!

Years later, when I took my first administrative role, I recalled how he created such a family type culture and I knew that was what I wanted to create as well. I almost felt like it was a call of duty to move into leadership and make the positive impact on others as he had done for so many years. Mainly because I remembered him telling me during my senior year that I was one of the most talented students he had ever had and that I needed to use those talents to reach my fullest potential. Although I haven't heard from him in years, I hope that our paths may still cross again one day, so I can let him know the influence that he had on my professional career.

Unfortunately, most principals today don't get years to put their imprint on a school like Mr. Kent was able to do. Gone are the days where a principal has years to build relationships, community, and a vision for the school. Instead, principals are hired to come in and make an impact immediately. With the expectations of making AYP, Race to the Top, and emphasis on high stakes testing, there is much more pressure on principals and all educational leaders to perform immediately. In fact, the turnover rate of educational leaders throughout the country is two to five years, depending on your position. With this type of turnover, how can anyone be successful?

What makes it even harder for a principal is that they're in a tug of war trying to balance the demands and expectations of the district and the needs and support of their teachers. In fact, I would say that being a principal might be one of the toughest and loneliest jobs in the world. Especially when you consider there is very little job security on top of everything else.

Because of the short window to perform, it is difficult for principals to take time to instill a vision, develop relationships, and create a positive culture. In my many interviews and own experience, I estimate that it can take up to three years to create a positive culture. However, principals typically have a year or less to make this kind of impact. Principals are thrown in the deep end of the pool and rather than a life vest, they are thrown an anchor and expected to keep everyone afloat! The catch-22 is that while principals need the relationships, positive culture, and clear vision to be successful, they aren't given the time to effectively develop them. Hence, we are not adequately preparing and supporting principals to succeed. Principals don't need more training in things like budgets, schedules, or even curriculum. In fact, you probably have staff with more experience and expertise in those areas. Principals need more development in actual leadership skills.

That's why *Principal Bootcamp* was written, to meet the needs of educational leaders in a high pressure, high expectations world. Leadership bootcamps are commonplace in the business world where key strategies are implemented at an accelerated pace to prepare leaders to lead from day one. This book is designed to provide you with the key strategies needed to connect with your staff, create a strong vision, and school culture from day one. In most instances, you may not even have a year to create such a culture, so these strategies will help you improve at an accelerated pace.

## Becoming a Person of Influence

Before you can influence others in your leadership capacity, you first have to understand what kind of leader you are because this will determine how you influence others. In fact, you cannot have influence over others until you have influence over self. When you become self-aware of how you lead, how you connect, and yes how you influence, then you are on your way to being an effective leader.

I have often said that **education has good administrators but poor leaders**. This is not a knock on principals but it is reflective of how we train our leaders for their role. Unfortunately, while education has made an effort to adapt to 21st-century learning, leadership has remained relatively unchanged since the industrial revolution. In fact, educational leadership was built upon the transactional (rewards versus punishment) leadership style that was developed during the industrial revolution, which is what most management or administration concepts are based upon. Since leadership influences culture, motivation, morale, and most aspects of school functioning, the fact that it has remained relatively unchanged could be a factor in why there are so many problems such as low teacher morale and high principal turnover.

Interestingly, the most commonly used leadership style is the **transactional style**. This style of leadership is based on the management style developed during the industrial revolution. This style focuses on setting objectives and goals for the followers, as well as the use of punishments/rewards in order to assure compliance with these goals. Unfortunately, this is also the least effective style of leadership but the one most closely aligned with the role of an administrator. When we think of ineffective leaders (and we have all worked for them at some point!), their hallmark was probably a compliance style of leadership because it is how they were trained. Even many programs are designated as education administration instead of leadership. This doesn't mean that transactional leadership is necessarily bad but because the focus is on controlling, organizing, and short-term planning, it is insufficient in maximizing the potential of the leader or the followers.

This style used by most administrators is effective in short-term and non-complex situations, relying on a system of reward and punishment to motivate followers. This style of leadership does not encourage innovation or creativity and is not effective in long-range planning in which input from staff is necessary.

While this style is common in schools, partly because there is such pressure to make quick changes, such as raising test scores, principals aren't given time to develop into effective leaders. Leaders cannot transaction their way into effective leadership or creating a positive culture for their staff. While not all transactional leaders are ineffective, this is definitely not the most productive or effective leadership style as it depends on influence of compliance. The hallmark of this style is usually "do as I say, not as I do."

Fortunately, your leadership style is not fixed. So, even if the administrator or transactional style is the one you are most accustomed to, doesn't mean that you can't change. In fact, most effective leaders have developed and grown into the Servant or what I call **selfless leadership style,** and you can too! This is the least common leadership style, but in many respects is the most effective and enduring leadership style. Becoming a selfless leader means that you **empower** your staff. The way to empower your staff is by focusing on their needs. **To empower others literally means to give up some of your own power**.

As a **selfless leader**, you must love to see people develop and thrive. I believe that when you operate out of a selfless leadership mindset and honestly help people grow personally you win their hearts. When this occurs, you have people who follow because they are committed to you and your vision and are not simply following to be compliant. This is what makes a dynamic team culture! As we leave this section, here are a few key traits that differentiate having an administrator (transactional) mindset and a selfless leader growth mindset. As you study the traits of the selfless leader, think of ways that you can begin implementing them. Choose to develop into a selfless leader!

| Administrator | Selfless Leader |
|---|---|
| ◆ Focus on systems/structure | ◆ Focus on people |
| ◆ Influenced by control/compliance | ◆ Influence by inspiring trust/commitment |
| ◆ Maintains status quo | ◆ Creates new status quo |
| ◆ Does things right | ◆ Does the right thing |
| ◆ Holds followers accountable | ◆ Accountable to followers |
| ◆ Manages | ◆ Leads |
| ◆ Asks how and when | ◆ Ask what and why |
| ◆ Imitates | ◆ Originates |
| ◆ Eye on bottom line | ◆ Eye on horizon |
| ◆ Short term focused | ◆ Long term focused |

Understanding your role as an influencer is the beginning of becoming an effective principal and creating a dynamic school culture! The key to a high performing school is an effective school leader. **You cannot administrate a school to excellence, but you can lead a school to excellence**. And let's be honest, becoming a selfless leader is not easy, or everyone would be one. It's also something that can't be faked. People know if you are being genuine or not. So, even though it's more work, it is worth the effort when you have a staff that trusts you and are committed to you. That is a staff that can accomplish great things!

**Leadership, after all, at its core is all about influence.** If your influence is because of your position or title then you create a culture where teachers are compliant out of fear or duty. If your influence is about connecting, empowering, and supporting, then your followers will be committed. The first step in creating a committed staff is to make a shift from an administrator mindset to a leader mindset.

## Bring Your Assets, Not Your Agenda

When you lead through the lens of a selfless leader, your whole perspective changes. You are no longer focused on what you can do for self, but what you can do for others. This doesn't mean that you don't have an agenda for the school, but it means that you aren't driven solely by a personal agenda. Case in point, I had an educational acquaintance who recently passed away. He was the principal of a middle school for many years and he was simply known as Mr. Z! One of the teachers recounted how Mr. Z would let the teachers bring their children to school each morning, so they would not have to rush to drop them off, or have their children waiting in their own school so early in the morning. He would then drive the students to the neighboring elementary school every morning and drop them off on time. While this was extra work for him, he didn't see it that way. He saw it as helping out his amazing staff. He put their needs first. He didn't have an agenda; he was simply using his assets to help out those he led. Think of the impact he had for teachers to remember his kind actions all these years later.

Many people who seek out leadership roles often have a personal agenda. They want to move up the ladder of success. In the business world, they call it climbing the corporate ladder. In the military, officers are trying to move up through the ranks. Moreover, in education, many are seeking the climb from the school level to the district level or what is often called the ivory tower or crystal palace. First, let me say that there is nothing wrong with being ambitious. If your desire is to be a principal and move up a superintendent one day, then there is certainly nothing wrong with following your dreams. However, if your focus is just on your personal agenda, you will never fully realize your ability to influence your staff and help them improve as staff or potential leaders.

Since this is called leadership bootcamp, a relatable story to this topic would be a conversation I had a couple of years ago with Captain Mike Abrashoff. He took the worst ship in the Navy, the USS Benfold, and made it the highest ship in the Navy during his tenure as Captain of the ship. In discussing his own rise in the military, he discussed how officers in the military are always looking for ways to advance their career. He said if you were at a formal gathering with a large crowd, someone may be talking to you but they were also scanning the room looking for someone of higher rank to go schmooze with because they were always looking for opportunities to get ahead. Having this attitude will make people feel like they are just pawns in your game rather than people you value and have their best interest at heart. This can lead to low morale, division of you versus them, and create a toxic environment.

**From day one, let your faculty know that you are bringing your assets not your agenda**. This means you use your assets to help your staff improve, develop, and succeed. So, what are your assets? Your assets in this case are your leadership strengths. Whether you are aware of them or not, everyone possesses talents and strengths. Some are more noticeable, like charisma, dominant size, or even high intellect. However, some of the greatest leaders have been introverts, small in size, and often had higher EQ (emotional intelligence) than IQ. For some leaders it may even be that you possess a certain positivity. I think we all can agree that we would rather work for someone who is positive and encouraging rather than someone who makes the Grinch look like Mother Theresa.

The key is to determine what talents and strengths you possess, develop them, and maximize them in your personal and professional life. And let's not forget that every expert in any field was once a novice, but they developed their strengths to excel. Take advantage of not just your assets, but your position as a leader to help those you lead. What is the purpose of leadership after all if it's not to help those you lead improve their own situation in some capacity? Use your assets to lift up those you lead, to bring them to a new level of leadership, service, and success in their own career.

## Reporting for Duty

Now that you have a better awareness of your leadership style and your focus as a leader, it is important to identify your entry strategy. Entry plans are designed to help individuals systemically collect information about the new context in which they are working. Leaders enhance their opportunities to be successful when they possess a deep and rich understanding of their work context.

Teachers and principals know that the first day of school is important in setting the stage for the year. Similarly, principals need a plan for the new school year. It is important to be clear about the vision for your school, the relationships within your school community that you want to nurture, the messages you want to communicate, and the priorities you will set for both you and your school. Specifically, a good entry plan includes goals such as:

1.  To establish and nurture positive and productive relationships with faculty, staff, parents, and community actively involved with the school.
2.  To learn the history, norms, culture, and climate of the school and community-at-large.
3.  To establish yourself as a listener and learner as well as a supportive and selfless leader.

The most important key to success, which will be reiterated throughout the book, is to **listen**. If you get the opportunity, visit your new school at the end of the school year before you take over the helm. This way, teachers and students will feel a sense of continuity. If this is not possible, then make plans to meet with staff and others as soon as possible over the summer. As you being to have conversation with administration, faculty, and staff, listen to what they are telling you.

Even though you are the leader, you are coming into their house and you want to honor their house. The worst thing you can do is spend your time talking and worst of all telling them what you are going to do. Initially, you are listening. As you listen to their stories and understand the culture of the school, then you can start preparing you vision, with their input in mind. Remember many of them will be there long after you, so make sure they have ownership in your vision. Here are a few key questions to focus on as soon as possible:

### School Goals

- ◆ What are the priority goals of the School Improvement Plan?
- ◆ What activities and work plans support these priority goals?

### Organizational Structures

- ◆ What are the committee and/or school structures of the school?
- ◆ How are roles and responsibilities identified and shared?
- ◆ How are decisions made? Who participates in decision-making?

### Communication Processes

- ◆ What structures exist to support coordination and articulation?
- ◆ How is information communicated across the school both vertically and horizontally?
- ◆ What are the specific ways individuals communicate in the building and with the community?

After you have listened and gained a better perspective of the school, its story, its people, and their culture of the school, only then can you begin to implement your plan and vision. **If you begin with your plan, it stays your plan, when you begin with their thoughts and input, it becomes "our" plan, and that makes all the difference in whether or not you will be successful**.

While we will examine how to implement your plan later on the book, the purpose of this section is simply your initial immersion into the school and building relationships with everyone before the first day of school. As we leave this section, remember to focus on the highest-impact activities that build relationships and give you information. Prioritize so that relationships come first. Yes, there's much work to do from day one, but people matter more. Don't forget that people have an innate need to connect before they are willing to go to battle for you.

## Develop Emotional Connectedness

While this section is neatly tucked away in the middle of the chapter, it is probably the most important qualifier to effective leadership. Why is emotional intelligence so important to leadership? Because you really can't be a selfless or servant leader without emotional intelligence. A leader's ability to engage people at the emotional level has emerged as the strongest indicator of leadership potential and performance. In fact, emotional intelligence (EQ) is a key hallmark of great leaders. So, to be a successful principal, your EQ may be the most important area of influence you have. Fortunately, if you don't have the highest EQ, it is something that can be developed, it will just require a little focus.

Think back to your favorite leader. Was it someone who was great at budgets, or did you say, "wow, this principal really knows how to create a schedule!" Probably not. In fact, it probably wasn't the management aspect of administration that inspired you, but it was the intangible things, such as feeling motivated, inspired, and even appreciated. These high EQ principals ask teachers things like, "How are you doing? How is the family? How can I help you?" They seek to connect with their staff on a personal level.

Some people are simply not good at the emotional aspect of leadership and these are also the people who tend to struggle in getting their staff committed to their leadership. It's important to remember that when dealing with humans, we aren't dealing with creatures of logic, but rather creatures of emotions. In fact, **most of the decisions we make are based on emotions**. We will try to justify our actions to others or ourselves with logic, but it is emotions that are the catalyst to our decisions and actions. So, remember how you display your emotions and how you connect with your staff's emotions will be the difference between success and failure. Remember when you make the emotional connections you capture their heart, because that is what will create a committed staff.

When it comes to emotional intelligence, you have to first control your own emotions. To be respected, principals cannot keep people guessing about how they will react to a particular situation. Principals who demonstrate erratic dispositions don't last long in the job. So, learning to control your emotions is the first step to building strong positive relationships with your staff. In fact, **until you learn to lead from within, you can't lead others**. While there are several factors in building high EQ, these four will accelerate your relationship connections most effectively.

**Self-awareness** is the ability to recognize your emotions and the effect of your moods on other people. The ability to recognize an emotion as it "happens" is the key to your EQ. If you evaluate your emotions, you can manage them. The major elements of self-awareness are emotional awareness and self-confidence. The place that leaders struggle the most is in self-awareness– understanding how people see them and what they really look like from the outside. We need to be self-aware. When you discover what you need to be doing differently, what you're poor at, that's what opens the door to improved performance. Because it allows you to put people in places of strengths where you may not be strong. So, self-awareness is key.

**Self-regulation** is the ability to manage disruptive emotions and impulses (fear, anxiety, anger, sadness); thinking before you act; taking responsibility for your actions. You often have little control over when you experience emotions. You can, however, have some say in how long an emotion will last by using a number of techniques to alleviate negative emotions such as anger, anxiety, or depression. A few of these techniques include recasting a situation in a more positive light, taking a long walk, and meditation or prayer. Self-regulation involves traits such as self-control, trustworthiness, conscientiousness, and adaptability.

**Empathy** is the ability to sense others' perceptions and feelings; seeing what others need to bolster their ability; listening to and validating the concerns of others. The more skillful you are at discerning the feelings behind others actions or reactions, the better you can control your reactions to them. An empathetic person excels at service orientation, developing others, and understanding others.

**Relationship intelligence** is the ability to understand the emotional fibers that make up others and to treat them accordingly; the ability to persuade, initiate change, and create group synergy. The development of good interpersonal skills is paramount to success in your life and career. In today's always-connected world, everyone has immediate access to technical knowledge. Thus, "people skills" are even more important now because you must possess a high EQ to better understand, empathize, and negotiate with others in a global economy. Among the most useful skills are influence, communication, conflict management, and building rapport.

This isn't to say that you need to be an overly emotional person to be a good leader, in fact wearing your emotions on your sleeve means that you probably don't have a high EQ. So, it's really more about managing emotions and understanding how to engage the emotions of those you lead to maximize results and commitment. I believe that to be an effective leader you have to learn to be **emotionally connected** rather than emotionally distant. Someone to whom people naturally gravitate. These are upbeat individuals who exude a positive vibe. Being emotionally connected creates a culture where your staff will **want** to give their best.

Emotional intelligence also translates to optimal outcomes as a leader. In challenging situations such as negotiations and terminations, or even in positive cases such as celebrations or achievements, a high degree of EQ can go a long way in building strong relationships and cementing your role as an effective leader.

## Be Fully Present

One of the most important attributes of an effective leader is to be **fully present**. Do not just be present, but be fully present. When you are at school you are physically present, but you also have a million things to do every day. You're rushed to a district meeting, you have a parent conference in the afternoon, a budget meeting, and the list goes on. You are always pulled and maybe feel like you don't have another minute to spare. So, while you may be physically present, you may not be mentally or emotionally present.

We always like to talk about being in the moment, but the reality is that that most people are only paying full attention in the present moment, 50 percent of the time. That means we basically miss out on half our life, with our attention somewhere other than in the moment.

Jeremie Kubicek, author of the book *5 Gears: How to Be Present and Productive When There Is Never Enough Time*, calls relational intelligence the future competitive advantage for leaders. Jeremie says, "Relational intelligence is the ability to connect and be present in the midst of tasks" (Kubicek, 2015). For instance, how many times have you been in a conversation with someone only to be distracted or to notice they are distracted? One example may be talking with someone who checks his phone or is replying to an email. This is not good relational intelligence. To be in the moment is to give someone your full attention.

And it's important to not only be in the moment, but to make sure you have the time to engage someone fully as well. As an administrator, have you ever had a teacher pop into your office to ask a question? A person with high relational intelligence may react to an interruption by saying: I would love to talk about this, but my mind is focused on something else at the moment and I'm not going to be fully with you right now. Can we meet at 2 p.m. when I can be fully focused on you? Being intentional, wanting to be present, that's relational intelligence. A teacher will respect your honesty and appreciate that you want to give them your full attention.

When you meet, then give them your full attention. Don't check email, take phone calls, check messages, or multi task. This is not only unprofessional but shows a lack of respect for the other person.

Here are a few strategies for increasing your relational intelligence or being fully present.

**Calmness**—I'm not anxious thinking about everything I need to get done, but instead just focus on enjoying the here and now. There's a real sense of peacefulness that comes from it.

**Clarity and focus**—I'm able to give my full attention to what I'm currently doing. Whether meeting with a parent, teacher, or the superintendent, being fully present allows me to not only do a better job, but to enjoy it more as well.

**More meaningful conversations**—When I'm fully participating in a conversation and truly taking the time to listen to what the other person has to say, I find that I always take something important away from the discussion. Whether it's a lesson or something I learned about the person, there is a lot to be gained from being present and actively engaged.

Finally, simply be focused on the moment. It can be easy to be on autopilot with your day-to-day schedule, but it is important to spice it up a bit each day so that you are able to actually enjoy the present. We are creatures of habit and often when we are in the "fray of the day" we turn on autopilot and in those instances we don't fully engage. Giving your full attention means you value the person or the activity. So, don't just seize the moment, but seize the fullness of it.

## Find a Mentor

Moving from an assistant principal position to a principal position is much like moving from a student teacher position into the role of lead teacher. Yes, you have experience, but when you hold the keys to the kingdom, it becomes a very different ball game. Even an experienced principal moving into a new school may experience new challenges and issues that they haven't encountered before and may have you looking for a mentor or at least a confidante with whom you can confide and bounce ideas.

The reality is that in the past principals were often thrown into the job with a sink or swim approach from the district level. This may be because they were treated the same way when they first became principals as well. However, with the high turnover rate and burnout rate of educational leaders, many districts have put formal mentoring programs into place. I know of several systems that have yearlong mentoring groups for new leaders in various roles, such as for AP's and for principals. These "cohorts" meet regularly, focus on topics such as leadership strengths, where they take tests like strengths finder, and they read and discuss leadership books.

Since leaving the K–12 setting to teach leadership at the graduate level, as well as speak and write on leadership, I have had the opportunity to connect with many leaders not just in education, but in the business world as well. I truly believe that good leadership is good leadership regardless of the field. But one of the things that drives effective leadership is good mentoring. Everyone is born with certain talents and strengths that can help them be more effective leaders, but never underestimate the importance of a quality mentor or mentors. I have several leaders that I mentor on a formal and informal basis. I usually meet with these individuals once a month for coffee and conversation. With those I mentor, we usually read a book and discuss topics like building relationships, empowering and developing followers into leaders. I enjoy books like *It's Your Ship* by Mike Abrashoff (2007), which is about his experience leading the USS Benfold. It has great stories, but has many great leadership tips and advice as well. Reading is an amazing mentoring tool all by itself. In fact, did you know the average CEO reads 60 books a year? They know the importance of not just getting to the top of the ladder, but staying on top of latest research, trends, ideas, etc. to remain on top.

If your district has a mentoring program, take full advantage of it. However, there is also nothing wrong with having a mentor or friend in another school that you can turn to if needed. Since great leadership is not confined to a certain field, find someone you trust, even if they aren't in education. Although you might believe that your experiences are unique, you will find that others have commonly experienced even the things that feel most personal to you. This also helps you know you're not alone or experiencing something unique. Choose an experienced principal as a mentor, someone who will listen, advise, and catch you before you jump off the proverbial cliff. Finally, a new principal, in fact every principal, needs a trusted colleague, friend, mentor, or confidante who can provide sage advice, listen to occasional venting, offer unwavering support, and, most important, bring laughter to the situation. All principals need someone supportive they can count on for difficult days. For that level of support, there is no substitute.

## Be Confident

One of the quotes I have used over the years is that "arrogance is NOT a leadership style." In fact, arrogance will turn off your staff faster than being inept. What is the difference you may ask? Well, **confidence** is grounded in experience and expertise with a sense of respect and humility; whereas **overconfidence** or **arrogance**, is grounded in little expertise and/or experience (it is unwarranted baseless **confidence** with lack of respect and humility).

As you can see there are major differences between being confident and arrogant. I think one of the key differences is humility. Have you ever met someone who probably should have been cocky or arrogant because of their success, but they were a down to earth type of person? I have been fortunate to meet famous celebrities, athletes, wealthy entrepreneurs, and the ones I liked the most were actually very humble people. I remember several years ago when I first met baseball hall of fame pitcher, John Smoltz. In one conversation, he shared that his goal was never to win a world series or be a Cy Young Award winner, although he accomplished both, but that his goal was to give up 200 homeruns.

Some may think that is a not a good goal, but when you really think about it, only a good pitcher is going to give up

200 homeruns. It would take years to give up that many, so a bad pitcher would never last long enough to give up 200 homeruns. John, at the height of his career, wasn't driving around a Lamborghini or Maserati, but instead drove around a BMW that was several years old. While I have several stories about people like John, who were very successful and confident, they weren't cocky or arrogant about it. In fact, they were very unassuming.

And if you are someone that is a bit overconfident, hopefully this is an area you reflect upon as you move into your leadership role. I will be honest that in my twenties, I was a very confident person and if I am totally honest, I was a bit cocky. I was national level bodybuilding competitor and I was an honors graduate. So, I felt like I was the man, and that I could take on the world. But that attitude tripped me up several times in my life and I realized that **arrogance is much worse for success than even ignorance**. Fortunately, I was a quick learner and learned to mix competence with an equal dose of humility. By the time I moved into my first leadership role, I realized leadership wasn't about me at all, but it was about the people I led. When you understand the selfless or servant aspect of leadership, you no longer seek the attention or admiration; you seek to help those you lead become successful.

I often use the analogy that a cocky leader spends much time looking into the mirror, while a humble leader spends much time looking through a window at others. This may not seem important to you, or maybe you are thinking, I am the leader now so I will lead how I want. Just be warned that if your staff sees you as cocky or arrogant, you will have a hard time connecting with them and getting them to buy into vision. Just remember that leaders need their followers more than their followers need them. Without them following, you aren't really a leader.

Before we leave this section, here are a few strategies to help you be more confident without being overconfident or arrogant.

1. **Be approachable**. Having confidence doesn't do you any good if you become standoffish or unfriendly

because of it. A pet peeve of so many teachers is that their administrators aren't easily approachable. Even if it's not because you are overconfident, it is usually mistaken for it.

2. **Be sincere**. Arrogant people either rarely offer compliments or do so in a way that feels forced and artificial, and it can almost undermine the success of the other person.

3. **Be humble**. Humility is different than vulnerability. Vulnerability can be used to get empathy, or be forced on a group, such as everyone asked to share a vulnerable moment, but this can actually have the opposite affect desired. But humility is genuine. It literally means showing a modest or low estimate of one's own importance It's not something that can easily be faked.

4. **Be willing to make and admit mistakes**. Overconfident people tend to oversell and under deliver. Don't be someone who thinks they know everything or even has to have an opinion on everything.

5. **Be forthcoming**. Be willing to openly share information. One of the biggest issues I see in schools is when information is held like its power. Only a few know certain things and it develops a divide in the staff.

6. **Share the success**. Another aspect of being confidence is to acknowledge others success and don't take all the credit yourself. There is nothing that kills morale faster than when an administrator takes the credit for the work of others. I worked for an administrator many years ago who was known for this and the staff had no respect for him. True leaders are generous with credit. They know that any great accomplishment takes many people and talents.

# 2

# Influencing Staff

## Building Relationships

As I mentioned in Chapter 1, I was fortunate enough to interview Captain Mike Abrashoff of the USS Benfold. His leadership style and story is one of the best examples of how culture influences a school or any organization. The story is basically how he took the worst ship in the Navy and transformed it into the best ship in the fleet by changing the culture of the ship.

In 1997, the USS Benfold had a change in leadership and a new captain, Mike Abrashoff, was to take over as commander of the ship. His first experience was the reception aboard the ship to bid the former captain farewell. The crew seemed glad and relieved that the former captain was leaving. It turns out that the former captain was a very intelligent man, but made the crew feel inferior and was condescending to them, which negatively affected the culture of the ship. The ship's performance was ranked last in the fleet and the crew didn't feel safe should they be called into action.

Abrashoff recalled (as quoted in Johnson & Sessions, 2016), "As I watched the ceremony that day and the reaction of the crew, I wondered to myself how the crew would react when I leave the ship after my tenure as captain?" He said this put things into perspective quickly for him. He knew his goal was to focus on improving the morale of the crew. He said,

> At this point in my career, other than sinking the ship, I knew I was set as far as retirement and even advancing in rank, so my goal wasn't to use the appointment to simply advance. Instead, I wanted to make a real difference in the crew of this ship.

Over the course of his tenure as captain, Abrashoff implemented many strategies, which helped build a positive culture. For instance, he created an environment where crew felt safe to take risks and take ownership in the crew's success. As Abrashoff replied, "I took responsibility for the actions of the crew, so they knew I had their back, even if they failed." Captain Abrashoff would also publicly praise the crew when they did good work—in fact, the crew affectionately named him "Mega Mike" because he would constantly praise his crew, which improved morale.

Sounding as much like a college coach as a ship captain, he said the reason that he felt like he needed to focus on the crew was that he wanted the parents of these young soldiers to be proud that their children were under his leadership. So, he didn't see them just as a crew, but he got to know them personally and found out their interests and their strengths, so he could best utilize their talents aboard the ship. Over the course of approximately two years, Abrashoff so profoundly changed the culture of the USS Benfold that it went from being the worst ship in the Navy to the best ship in the fleet.

Interestingly, as his time as captain came to an end, he decided that he didn't want the traditional pomp and circumstance given to such an auspicious occasion, but rather he had 310 lobsters flown in for the last dinner with his crew. As he said, "I knew many of them had never seen, much less eaten a lobster." Then, the next morning, rather than the traditional ceremony, which he had experienced when coming on board, he simply gathered his crew around him on deck in their working coveralls, and gave what is the shortest change of command speech in military history. He simply told them, "You know how I feel." He said he left that day with pride, not so much for making the ship the best in the Navy, although that was great, but that he left an accomplished, tight-knit, effective crew that he was unabashedly proud to have commanded.

After the interview with Abrashoff, I realized that as a leader he influenced the culture of the ship, just as the captain before him had influenced the culture of the ship, as well. Under the leadership of one captain, the ship and crew were seen as the worst in the Navy, and yet, with different leadership and a positive change in culture, the same crew became the best ship in the fleet.

I can think of no better example of just how important culture plays in the functioning of an organization, and how important leadership is in influencing the culture. Mainly because you have to work with the staff that is there. You can't bring on your own new team of teachers and administration. The school you are at may be the lowest performing school in the district, state, or nation, but that doesn't mean that with effective leadership it can't be turned around! Whether the school has a poor culture, poor test scores, or even low morale, you can turn the Ship around. Just like with Captain Abrashoff, you may find the poor results were really just a by-product of a bigger problem, the relationships between leader and staff.

## Life in the Trenches

Now that you have a better idea of your own leadership strengths and the importance of your influence, it is now time to focus on the most important aspect of leadership and that is the influence you have on the people you lead. As I mentioned in the Chapter 1, being other-focused is one of the hardest things we do as humans. It is human nature to be selfish, to focus on our own comfort and ourselves comes very easy. But as a leader, you have to focus on the needs of those you lead. If there's one thing I never forgot when I moved into my first leadership role was what it was like in the trenches. It influenced the decisions I made, how I treated teachers and my expectations of them. Having walked a mile in their shoes helped me empathize and relate to their needs. Never forget what it was like as a teacher and be the administrator that helps them be their best self.

Getting people on board with your leadership may be the toughest part of leadership. For leaders to lead, they not only need exceptional talent, but the ability to attract followers. Regrettably, with high principal turnover, it's becoming harder to get people to follow because they don't want to buy in if the next leader is just around the corner. So, if we are looking for the **3R's** most needed for a principal to be effective, it is **Relationships, Relationships, Relationships**! The best way to build those relationships is to get into the trenches with your staff. While trenches may sound harsh for teaching, but as Sargent Shriver observed during the speech he delivered on October 13, 1972, as part of his vice presidential campaign with George McGovern, "teaching was the hardest job in America." I would say that statement is truer today than ever. Teachers know while their job is fulfilling it is uniquely hard because it is physically, mentally, and emotionally exhausting. So, teachers want someone who has been in their shoes, who can appreciate their struggles, and even more, who is willing to jump back into the trenches with them.

I remember once when one of the boy's bathrooms flooded and I jumped right in with the custodians to mop up the floors. I didn't think it as a job beneath me but a problem that required immediate resolution. This isn't a pat on the back for me, but rather an opportunity for you to see that there really is no job too small regardless of your role when the need arises. I wasn't just in the trenches, but in the latrine trench, literally! Teachers appreciate leaders who don't think of themselves as too big to do small things. This is actually endearing to most teachers and shows that you are about the people not your position. **Teachers don't want someone telling them how to navigate the trenches; they want someone in the trenches leading them**.

## Building Trust

Imagine a staff that trusts you to buy into your vision for the school. It's easy to say yes I will follow, but are they really willing to do whatever it takes to fulfill the mission of the school? I am reminded of the story of Charles Blondin (Abbott, 2011). You may have never heard of him, but Blondin was a world-famous tight-rope walker. Early in 1859, Blondin decided that he would be the first to walk a tightrope stretched across Niagara Falls, 1,100 feet long and 160 feet in the air. There were thousands of people gathered around. Some to heckle, some to cheer, and some just to say they were there.

As Blondin arrived, he got the crowd worked into a frenzy, and then jumped up on the rope and had a couple of warm up exercises. To the crowd's amazement, he didn't look nearly as stable on the rope as he should. Parts of the crowd began to jeer and hurl insults and laugh at the guy that was about to fall to his death. Shouts of "This can't be done," "you'll never pull this off," blah blah blah. The rest of the crowd grew silent. Blondin continued. Blondin grabbed his balancing pole and started down the rope. The entire path across he seemed to stumble and trip. The entire crowd grew quiet. Not a peep. As Blondin reached the other side, he knew he had their attention when they went from dead silent to offering a thunderous applause.

He arrived back to everyone cheering. He had done it, but he wasn't done. He then proceeded to go back and forth another five times. He traversed the rope with no pole. Then he took a chair halfway and sat for a spell. Then he took some juggling pins and juggled all the way across, and then took a hot plate and made himself lunch. With every trip, the crowd became louder.

Then a wheelbarrow was unveiled. The crowd cheered and there was no doubt in his ability to move it across. Blondin quieted the crowd, and you could hear a pin drop. He then asked for a volunteer . . . to ride in the wheelbarrow . . . across Niagara Falls. The crowd had seen him in action, they believed him, but they didn't trust him, at least not with their lives. The only person who was willing to get into the wheelbarrow was his manager. His manager knew how good he was and trusted him. They made the trip across and back safely to the roar of the crowd.

While this is a great story, it also provides some lessons relating to trust, risk taking, and even teamwork. When you try something big, there will be supporters, but there may be people who hope you fail. When you try big things, it will more than likely be the people who trust you and who you have built relationships with that are willing to hop into the wheelbarrow with you. You don't want spectators on your team; you want participators who trust you and your vision.

Relationships begin with trust. There needs to be trust in leadership, in relationships, and even in the established process. Principals must be prepared to engage collegially with teachers in ways that are consistently honest, open, and compassionate, while also dependably demonstrating sound knowledge and competent decision making associated with administering academic programs.

The old adage you never get a second chance to make a first impression is never truer than when it comes to trust. They are scrutinizing, critiquing, and judging you to see if you are up to the task. We typically think it takes time to build trust, but the reality is that in that first impression people try to answer the question, "Can I trust this person?"

If someone you're trying to influence doesn't trust you, you're not going to get very far; in fact, you might even elicit suspicion because you come across as manipulative or you may seem threatening. Trust begins with caring. Make sure your focus is on your staff, and you gain their trust within a few weeks rather than months.

One way to build trust is to show trust. I remember early in my teaching career working for a principal who required teachers to sign in each morning. He did this because a couple of teachers were consistently late. Rather than address the issue with them personally, he would just make sweeping policy changes. Don't make sweeping rule or policy changes that everyone has to comply with even though there was no reason to include them. This is a terrible way to lead. Making teachers sign in was demoralizing and created a sense of mistrust rather than trust. I never forget this and when I moved into a leadership role and I never made my staff sign in or sign out. My only expectation was that they be in their classroom to greet their students as they arrived each morning and that they didn't rear-end the buses when they left in the afternoon! I knew they were professionals and should be treated as such. If there was an issue, I dealt with it individually, which will see how to do in the section on handling conflict. Treating teachers with respect and as professionals, goes a long way toward creating a level of trust that will benefit you and them.

If you are a principal moving into a new school, you may be coming into a situation where trust has been lost. That's why it's so important to have that entry plan we discussed previously, because you want to be prepared to put in extra work in the trust area if needed. Trust is the glue that holds a team together and gives you some gravitas or leeway when implementing new ideas, because they trust you have their best interests in mind, or at least the best interest of the school. This does not mean they will following you blindly or won't have questions or concerns, but it will give you the benefit of the doubt. It's like I always told my teachers,

> you're entitled to get answers to every question you have. . . . That doesn't mean you're going to like the answers. But it's going to be truthful, and I know you can deal with the truth. This might even create additional questions, but we'll get through them as well and we always did!

So what are some of the keys to building trust? While there are many strategies to do this, some of which will be addressed later, here are:

### Five Ways to Earn Your Staff's Trust Quickly
1. **Listening.** There is nothing more important to building relationships and influencing others than to listen. Teachers need to feel heard. This means leaders show empathy and truly seek to understand the challenges and requests from teachers. Listening is all it takes to others they are important.
2. **Share your story.** Before you hit the ground running with curriculum, lesson plans, and vision, share your story with your staff. For example, share with your staff who you

(your family) are and how you got into education. This transparency will go a long way toward developing trust.

3. **Develop shared purpose.** Teachers and principals should have many similar goals, which can create a shared purpose, but we often experience our differences with more emotion than our similarities. We all want students to learn, we want a safe environment, and we want a positive culture. If you give teachers input into the vision of the school, they will be more likely to believe you value and support them. Which is an instant trust builder!

4. **Authenticity.** Teachers want their leaders to be authentic. Authentic leaders reveal who they are and show what they value. They are self-aware and express their thoughts and feelings in healthy, caring ways. Show your employees you care about them and get to know them personally in and outside of school.

5. **Exhibit warmth.** Research indicates that the effective way to influence, and to lead, is to begin with warmth, as it is this quality that facilitates trust and the effective communication and acceptance of ideas. Prioritizing warmth helps leaders to connect immediately with colleagues— demonstrating that they understand them, and can be trusted by them.

As we close this section, never forget that **relationships are built on trust**. If you don't give teachers responsibilities, a voice in the process, or if you micromanage them, they will assume you don't trust them. If they don't feel trusted, they will never trust you & strong relationships will never be built. **There is no relationship without trust**.

## Be Approachable

I have often said that teaching is the toughest job in America, but being a principal is the loneliest job in America. You are in a tug of war between the expectations of the districts and the needs of your staff. Sometimes you may feel like you are an island unto yourself. As a principal, you always want to exhibit profession-alism and to treat your staff professionally. In fact, most teachers would love an administration to treat them as professionals! But, this doesn't mean you can't be personable and approachable, you are dealing with humans after all.

This is especially important when you're the principal. If you isolate yourself, or try to build your perceived authority by dis-tancing yourself from the others, it might only serve to alienate you and put you in a position where you're viewed with dis-trust or even resentment. This doesn't mean you're trying to be their buddy, because they want a leader, not another friend, but it doesn't mean that you shouldn't be friendly. Approachability is having other people feel comfortable bringing either good news or bad news and having their leader listen to them.

So, go out of your way to have personal exchanges with your employees and co-workers. You don't need to build friendships, but there's no reason why you can't get to know each other. Personal working relationships are important for cultivating a sense of team, and if people see you as another person on the team, they'll be more receptive when you disclose your ideas or opinions. The key here is to seem imperfect, approachable, and human. Some of the ways I kept that approachable side was to always inquire about events in my teachers' lives. If a child or family member was sick or maybe someone was graduating or getting married, I would ask about them. Teachers appreciate it when you treat them as humans with lives outside of school, and not just the teacher in the classroom.

Being approachable also involves your verbal and even non-verbal cues. I remember visiting a school once where the prin-cipal, a friend of mine, had a stern expression on his face for most of the visit. His expression wasn't warm and inviting even though he is a great guy and has a good sense of humor. He just seemed to be stressed and it showed in his expressions. I suggested that he smile more because it would make him feel better and that it would help people be more comfortable approaching him. Smiling is approachability 101.

When I mentor leaders now, I like to share the phrase from the old television program *Fantasy Island*. When the plane would land on the island, the host, Mr. Roake would be there with the staff to greet the new guests and he would always say, "Smiles everyone, smiles!" Let that be your motto as well. In fact, did you know a smile makes you look more attractive and approachable? One of the most common responses when I talk to teachers about approachability of their administrators is that they always have a serious look on their face and act like they are always running late somewhere. They often don't even say hello in the hallway. Regardless of how busy you are, always take time to smile, say hello, and be approachable. As we leave this section, keep the following seven points in mind and watch the difference it makes with your staff.

1. Don't pretend to know it all. They know you don't so this mindset makes you appear disingenuous and unapproachable.
2. Share stories to connect. It can be a story of struggle, failure, or triumph. Just connect.
3. Admit when you're wrong. Nothing is more authentic than a person in a position of power admitting they did something wrong. Make mistakes, just not excuses.
4. Remember what it was like as a teacher and how your experiences may help them. And remember to jump in the trenches with them as much as possible.
5. Have a sense of humor. You work in a building full of students, so smiling and laughing are a prerequisite. Smiles everyone, smiles!
6. Take time to ask staff about life events.
7. Never be so rushed that you don't make eye contact in the halls or greet staff and students as you pass them.

## Meet Staff

As a principal new to a school, there will be many demands on your time during your first few weeks there. Everyone will want to meet the new principal and discuss their own agenda, whether it's ideas they have, issues they have, or just to get a read on you as a leader. In order to successfully launch your principalship, focus on building the relationships you'll need to be successful. Those critical to the first few weeks of school will be your faculty and staff.

Welcoming teachers to meet with you individually or in small groups during summer can build relationships that the rush of the school year doesn't always allow for. This is where you can put their minds at ease and let them know that you are a leader worth following. That you have their best interests in mind, and that you want to build a dynamic team culture. When meeting with your staff initially, don't focus on your vision or plans. In fact, you should listen more than you talk the first time you meet those with whom you will work. You can even send out a staff survey to get feedback before you meet with them and use the information to begin the conversation.

During your meetings, ask guided questions and then LISTEN. Meeting with your staff is not one of those "get to it as time allows" tasks, so make it a priority. One of the best ways to make your staff feel valued and to start building relationships is for them to see that they are your priority. Also, how can you get the most out of your staff if you don't know what talents and strengths they bring to their role and to the school?

**Schedule meetings with your teachers**. While it would be ideal to meet with your faculty and staff at once to introduce yourself, that may prove difficult during the summer. If it's not possible then don't wait until preplanning to meet with them, but instead meet with teachers individually or with departments or teams as soon as possible. Your goal is to get to know a little bit about each of the teachers in your building.

While this may seem like a time-consuming activity, it is very beneficial to connecting with your faculty. During this meeting, you can ask them to share their thoughts on what has been working and not working, as well as overall school culture. This activity not only builds interpersonal relationships with the staff, but also provides you with valuable insights in order to develop your game plan. Also, try to remember as many names as possible and use their name continually. People love the sound of their own name.

**You should also meet with the office staff to discuss office operations and your expectations for the office tone and climate**. I have often said that you can tell how effective a principal is by watching and listening to the office staff when you enter a school. They are also the first impression people experience on entering the school. A friendly, helpful, and competent attitude goes a long way in making a great impression with families, students, and other staff. Taking the time to meet with them and learning how the office operates will pay great dividends for you. Once you understand the office operations and current culture of the front office, then you can share your expectations for the tone and operation of the office.

## The Right Questions

The best leaders know that in order to truly be effective and successful you must do one thing really, really well … ask good questions. And it doesn't stop there. You must not only be asking great, thought provoking questions, but listening requires asking the right questions. Asking questions of your staff is a great way to show them you value their opinion and expertise, such as asking them their input on curriculum or textbooks.

But, the **two** most important questions that you can ask are: **How are you doing? How can I help you?** These two questions show that you care about them not just as teachers, but as humans as well. The key is that when you ask these questions, then you have to listen, really listen. If you aren't listening to the ideas and needs of your staff, how can you possibly serve them?

**How are you doing** may seem like a simply question, but asking at the right time can make a big difference. Caring for those you lead is a trademark of a selfless/servant leader. Pay attention to your staff and look for signs that they may be struggling. Did you know our faces are the best places in which to read our emotions? It's a window to how we're really feeling. Learning to recognize those micro-expressions of feeling allows us to connect more fully with others. Respectfully recognizing another's emotional state will allow you to know when to ask them how they are doing.

Now most of us have been conditioned to ask that question without really expecting more than the obligatory response of "I am fine." In fact, it has become so desensitized that no one really listens to the reply. So, you may have to take it a step further to recondition your staff that you really want to know how they are. You may have to start by asking questions like "how is everything with your family?". Moving the conversation away from the classroom and making it more personal may catch their attention. Even if it takes a little time to get them to open up, don't give up.

When you have built good relationships with your staff, you can tell when someone is having an off day. If you have a teacher who is always smiling, outgoing, and happy, but all of the sudden they seem worried, preoccupied, or stressed out, make sure to check on them. Some staff members may not want to share issues, but when you ask sincerely, they may open up to you. There may be an illness in the family or they may even be struggling with a health issue. And not that you need all the details, but knowing there is an issue provides you with the ability to help out if possible. Do they need a class covered to take a child to the doctor, or do they maybe need to come in later for a few days because of a family emergency? Never be afraid to ask how someone is doing, make sure you listen, and then take action if needed.

Which leads us into the other important question, **how can I help you**. Nothing reflects a servant or selfless leadership more than "how can I help you?", or "how can I serve you?". This question is an expression of humility and support. It should almost be the ending to all your interactions with your staff. I think leaders who pose this question have an understanding of the power of service.

As a leader, it is important to have your pulse on the morale, stress levels, and environmental conditions of your teachers, so you can calm high stress situations, or inspire when spirits are waning. You need to be especially mindful of their full plates and recognize key stress time. Don't overload teachers with professional development during report card season. Don't expect committee work or other duties during conference time. Avoid new initiatives and stresses during the end of the term, report-writing periods, or while teachers are grading exams. If there's any way you can lend a hand during these times, whether it's taking on some of the work yourself, or covering a teacher's lunch supervision shift, help shoulder the load for your team.

However, when you ask the question "how can I help you?", listen, and then be ready to roll up your sleeves and go to work. I know that I personally have rolled up my sleeves many times and jumped into the trenches. I have helped cover classes when a teacher needed to leave early, helped clean up the cafeteria when they were short staffed, and I have helped move more classrooms than I care to remember. Some of these teachers never let go of anything! But when your staff sees that you are sincere and truly there to serve them, then you have captured their heart. Ask the right questions, really listen, and then respond. You will have a staff willing to literally go to battle with you.

## Administration of Appreciation

As I travel and speak to leaders and mentor leaders, one of the points I emphasize is to put teachers first. I wrote a book on the topic titled, *Putting Teachers First*, which has become my mantra for the past several years. When you show your staff that you support and appreciate them, they are willing to do just about anything for you.

If you happen to be a leader who thinks adults don't need appreciation, here is a study that may change your mind. A 10-year, 100,000-person study conducted throughout the U.S. and Canada by the O.C. Tanner Institute and HealthStream (Sturt & Nordstrom, 2014) confirms that recognition and appreciation tops the list of things employees say they want most from their employers. According to the study (Sturt & Nordstrom, 2014), 79 percent of employees who quit their jobs cite a lack of appreciation as a key reason for leaving. And of the people who report the highest morale at work, 94.4 percent agree their managers are effective at recognizing them. Now imagine if principals focused on the morale of their staff?

When I was a teacher, I can't tell you how many times I heard a principal use the term, "the students come first" to justify implementing a program or to quiet any pushback on an idea or initiative. The reality is that yes, the students come first to the teacher, but to the principal, the teacher should come first. In my book, I point out that effective leaders in business suggest that their customers don't come first, but that their employees come first, because if they take care of their employees then they know their employees will take care of them. The same is true in education. When teachers feel like they are valued, supported, and made a priority by their administration, then they work that much harder to take care of their students. In fact, when teachers feel valued and that their strengths are being used, they are six times more effective! Imagine what could be accomplished if teachers were **six times more engaged and effective**! It can be a game changer!

The reality is that students should not be the only reason a teacher loves their job, but administrators should be one of the major reasons too! Create a school culture where teachers want to be there! Not just for the kids, but for you too. Since this may be a new concept for you, you may be asking, well Brad, how can I make teachers a priority? Great question! I have interviewed and surveyed thousands of teachers over the years and here are a few key points to remember:

- ◆ Don't add to teachers' plates without first taking something away.
- ◆ Make them part of decisions that affect them and their students.
- ◆ Appreciate the effort that teachers put in and have the respect to acknowledge the staff.
- ◆ Make sure you provide support, encouragement, and appreciation.
- ◆ Be present. Make yourself available to them.
- ◆ Make sure planning time is sacred. Not used for covering classes or excessive meetings.

◆ Encourage self-care. Make sure teachers aren't working consistently long hours.

◆ Respect your staff for their expertise and experience.

While there are hundreds of ways to focus on teachers such as pay increases and more resources, the reality is that you are limited in what you can actually do. You can begin with this list and try to address them as the year progresses. However, two of the most common responses that have a high priority for teachers concern autonomy and innovation. If you begin your year letting teachers know that you respect their expertise and professionalism, you will have a group of teachers who will be do everything in their power to show you that you made the right choice.

**Autonomy** is our desire to be self-directed. It increases engagement over compliance. Effective teachers like to feel that they are seen as the experts. The way to make stars out of teachers is to let teachers be stars. Let them be an example of innovation, to let them find the path that works best for them and their students, even if sometimes this means failure. If they are allowed to search for the best methods or answers, guess what, they'll find them.

Autonomy can also be viewed as the freedom to develop collegial relationships among their peers to accomplish tasks. This means teachers don't necessarily see autonomy as walking into the classroom, closing the door, and doing whatever they want, but that it means they work with colleagues to create, develop, and implement strategies to improve teaching and learning. Collegiality can be expressed through experiencing challenging and stimulating work, creating school improvement plans, or even leading curriculum development.

Curiosity is the foundation of **innovation**. We open new doors and new ideas and keep moving forward. And it begins with administration. Are teachers motivated more by a leader who constantly tells them what to do or one who poses questions? Or better yet, allows them to pose questions? As we mentioned before, there is no other field where innovation and curiosity are more important than in education. We want students to develop a curiosity for learning and to develop their talents to be innovators who contribute to society. Well, the best way to get students curious and innovative is for teachers to reflect it. Teachers are more willing to exhibit these traits when they have administrators who encourage them to be innovative. Motivating staff comes in many shapes and sizes.

Often, the most simple and effective ways are overlooked. I truly believe in the power of finding new methods and resources, exposing staff to these best practices, and giving them the green light to try it out in their educational spaces. Students take risks when they see teachers take risks. Teachers take risks when they see school and district leaders take risks. Supported risk-taking helps contribute to a healthy school environment. It's what motivates and keeps educators passionate about the important work they do on a daily basis. So, innovation is about taking these calculated risks and not being afraid to fail. We want students to have the confidence to take risks and be curious and innovative. But, how can they if teachers aren't motivated to try new and creative ways of reaching the students? Is your school culture a catalyst for innovation? It's important to listen to your teachers, listen to their ideas, and build a space of trust and openness that allows everyone to feel comfortable and encouraged to come forward with new ideas. Ultimately, it is about building **trust** in your staff to take risks in a safe environment.

The essence of putting teachers first is that you see them as professionals and experts in their fields. Yes, you motivate, inspire and support them in their pursuit, but if you truly trust them and allow them to use their talents, then you will give them the freedom to be excellent. When you put teachers first, they will know you have their back and that gives them the comfort to try big things, to swim in the deep end, to make a real difference!

## Be Visible

In the military, AWOL means Absent without Leave. Based on the circumstances, it can result in a fine and confinement, or even lead to a discharge. In leadership, AWOL could be defined as Absent without Leader. For some teachers this is a good thing and they relish when their principal isn't in the building. But, that should not be the case. You should have such a great relationship with your staff that they want you to be present and accounted for!

The reality is that one of the most important attributes of a leader is that they are actually present. How odd would it be if you went to the orchestra and the conductor wasn't on stage? How would the music sound? Or what if a football team started a game without their coach? Would they know what to do? While you DO NOT want to micromanage your staff, you do want to be there to support and mentor your team.

It's hard to be invisible if you are in the trenches with your team as much as possible. Remain visible and approachable through the school day. The principal should NOT be hard to find. Instead of being tucked away in the office, be out in the school. Be in the hallways to interact with teachers and students throughout the day. This may not seem like a good use of time, but it is more important than you think. From the teacher's perspective, the principals that lead are the principals that are seen.

Greet students and their parents in the morning as they arrive and get out of cars or greet students as they step off the bus. Chat with the parents and bus drivers. Ask good questions, then listen and learn from the responses. Ask about needs, potential problems, or brewing issues. While showing visibility, the multitasking principal at the same time demonstrates concern for others' welfare. That time invested in collecting information can prevent concerns from escalating and trouble from developing. You may find out about a student who may be having issues or is experiencing family problems. A proactive leader can head off a lot of situations before they become problems by simply being present.

Teachers and students alike need to feel like their school administrators are active members of the day-to-day school community. You provide a sense of safety, security, normalcy, and even calmness in a chaotic world. Here are a few more ideas of how to be seen throughout the day, while positively influencing the school culture.

- ◆ Make morning announcements. This is a great time to recognize accomplishments, celebrate successes, catch people being good, provide necessary information, and establish expectations. For children, the principal's voice conveys security, stability, and reassurance.
- ◆ Cover for a teacher. Offering your services as a guest teacher to model techniques and engage with students.
- ◆ Be available in the hallways during transition times.
- ◆ Serve food in the cafeteria. Help serve food or pass out milk during lunch. Observe kids' behavior in a less structured environment. Reinforce your expectations of manners and cooperation and that you are a servant leader.
- ◆ Join different groups of staff and students for lunch. Listen, learn, and get a pulse for what is happening in the school.
- ◆ Attend extra-curricular events. Let students know you care about them all as a person and not just a student. Be there to support them as they show off their passions and talents.
- ◆ Frequent the playground. What a great opportunity to see students in their natural habitat, running, playing, and having fun. This is also a great time to take a walk and chat with students who may need a little extra attention or may be struggling.
- ◆ Sit in on professional development sessions. Show your staff that PD is important and that you're part of the team and willing to grow and learn as well.

Sometimes, just the simple fact that an administrator makes the effort to be present throughout the building can be enough to proactively prevent issues before they have a chance to occur. Be visible in hallways/classes more than office. But don't let your only visits be when you do evaluations; make it regular so they see you're invested in learning process. In specials' classes too! This means you are **staying in touch with issues and concerns of individuals in the school**.

## Maslow Before Bloom

We've heard a lot lately about Maslow before Bloom when it comes to our students, but guess what, when it comes to teachers, they need Maslow before Bloom as well. Teachers need to feel safe, like they belong, and that their emotional needs are met. While it is everyone's responsibility to create a positive and supportive school culture, the principal is the thermostat who sets the climate for the school environment. This is where you can build equity with your staff. Well, there's no better investment than leaders willing to build positive relationships with their staff.

First, put your staff at ease. An approachable leader makes people feel comfortable and at ease. People at ease can work together, connect, and communicate without fear of retribution. I remember one principal I had early in my career who would purposely send vague emails to teachers to meet at the end of the day. Teachers would be worried the rest of the day about the meeting, even if they had done nothing wrong. The principal said he did it because he wanted to keep teachers on their toes. I can't imagine treating teachers so unprofessionally. I would rather have teachers feel at ease than to have them worried about some mind games. Learn to be kind, gentle, and caring to your staff. Even if this doesn't come easy to you, it is something that you can develop much like your emotional intelligence. They are professionals, after all, who pour their heart and souls into their job, so be mindful of this and make sure you let them know how much you appreciate their commitment.

Teachers by nature speak the language of affirmation. This is why most teachers call their job a calling as much as a profession. So move beyond seeing them based on their titles or roles and see them as human who also need affirmation. As leaders, it's easy for our focus to be on what we want to accomplish or what matters most to us. Unfortunately, this can lead us to treat our employees as more of a means to an end than valued contributors to our schools vision or long-term goals. Teachers in reality are your most valuable resource. You need to care of them.

Remember to do the little things like learn their names quickly. Ask about their children, family, or even their pets. People love to talk about themselves and the people important to them. And remember to ask them the two key questions often: How are you? How can I help you? I hope that by now you realize just how powerful those two questions can be. These will keep communication lines open and give you the opportunity to really listen and help.

It is important to have a warm demeanor, kind words, and down to earth approach rather than be disarming and encouraging. It also means you are caring and compassionate. When teachers realize you truly care about them, then you have captured their trust. This is the highest level of connection that you can obtain in the workplace.

It may not be surprising that those who perceive greater affection and caring from their leaders or even colleagues perform better. A study published in the *Harvard Business Review* (Shafer, 2018), showed that employees who felt they worked in a loving, caring culture reported higher levels of satisfaction and teamwork. They showed up to work more often. The research also demonstrated that this type of culture related directly to improved mood, quality of life, and overall satisfaction.

The more love teachers feel at school, the more engaged they are. This companionate love, which is far less intense than romantic love is based on warmth, affection, and connection rather than passion. It is the small moments such as a warm smile, a kind note, a sympathetic ear day after day, month after month, that help create and maintain a strong culture of companionate love and the staff satisfaction and commitment that comes with it.

# 3

# Influencing Teams

Lee Iacocca was one of the most successful business leaders of the 20th century, especially in the auto industry. He took the Chrysler Corporation from the brink of bankruptcy and made it one of the most profitable automobile companies at the time. He only took $1.00 in salary the first year just to show his commitment to his leadership. He was also the first executive to put assembly line workers on the board of a major corporation. Now that is empowering others! But he is probably best remembered for his attitude toward hiring, about which he said, "I hire people smarter than myself and then get out of their way" (Iacocca, 1986).

He understood that surrounding yourself with the best people, building the best team, is what leads to success. He understood leadership wasn't about his power, but empowering those he led. Empowering others should be your goal as well. This may be the toughest aspect of leadership because let's be honest for a moment, it's much easier just to tell people what to do and then make sure they do it. It's easier to make sweeping rules that keeps everyone in line than to trust people to do the right thing because one or two people may not always follow rules. And we would rather everyone be just a little miserable and compliant than to be dealing with people who may challenge the process. Yes, that might sound easier, but this is not the environment you want to lead in and definitely not the environment where you will get the most out of your staff. This type of leadership creates a culture of compliance instead of commitment. There is little chance of creating a high performing school where staff morale is low and there is a compliance-focused culture.

Hire good people and get out of their way. This doesn't mean you are not leading, but you're creating a collaborative team culture where everyone is valued and has a voice. In a five-year study of 180 schools, a team of researchers found that nearly all of the staff working in high-performing schools had more influence over school decisions than did staff from low-performing schools (Seashore Louis, Leithwood, & Anderson, 2010). Their research indicated that collective leadership, if organized and managed effectively, has a greater impact on outcomes than any one individual can. This means if you are willing to trust your teachers with more responsibility, autonomy, and freedom, you can create a winning team. High performing schools aren't built on only the work of a good leader, but on the work of a great team led by a great administration!

So how do we build a great team? It begins with you, the school leader. A team with effective leadership will always do better than a team with no set roles, plans, or a direction. I often equate the principal and staff as an orchestra. The principal puts the right people in the right places and then leads them as they create masterpieces. The orchestra analogy also reinforces the focus of a team working in **collaboration instead of isolation.**

Principals with a servant-leadership style set up a structured schedule to collaborate on classwork and goals in the classroom. They support teachers by offering advice and mediating between individuals to focus on setting up an effective strategy for student education.

Collaboration is a crucial component when it comes to developing an effective school. When a school district wants to improve and enhance student performance, it must start with the growth of the teachers and staff. By setting up a collaborative environment, the school will see improvements as teachers learn from the experiences of their peers. A principal plays an essential role in the process because they must facilitate the collaboration and encourage discussion while offering support to teachers and students.

## Team Chemistry

You may be thinking that you already have teams. For instance, we make use of grade level teams such as a 5th grade team. This grouping defines the team (everyone teaches the same grade), but it doesn't necessarily explain why it exists. A purpose for being a grade-level team could be, "We are a team of teachers who support each other, share ideas, learn from each other, and identify ways that we can better meet the needs of our 5th grade students." It's important to be clear on a team's purpose and goals.

Building a team is not about a group of people working in the same building or serving together on committees, but is about creating a dynamic organism that has the same goals and is there to support each other in the achievement of those goals. The **main difference** between group and team is that **the members of a group share common characteristics** whereas **members of a team share a common goal or purpose**. And an effective team has team chemistry which helps create high performing school cultures. Here are a few key differences between a group mentality and team mentality in your school (Figure 3.1, NDT Resource).

As you can see, there are some important distinctions between groups and a team. The team is much more relationship focused. Teams understand that they have influence beyond their classroom, that they aren't working in isolation, and that everyone works together. The highest performing schools have teachers who understand that these are all our kids (not just "the ones I teach"), and that we are in this together. When it is the "I" mentality and not the "team" mentality, teachers don't see faculty meetings as important, they don't see giving input for decisions to be necessary, and they may feel like they are competing against other teachers.

## GROUP  VERSUS  TEAM

| GROUP | TEAM |
|---|---|
| Group refers to a number of people who are connected by some shared activity, interest, or quality | Team refers to a number of persons associated together in work or activity |
| May not share a common goal | Share a common cause or goal |
| Specific roles and duties are not assigned to individuals | Specific tasks are assigned to each individual |
| Members are interdependent | Members are interdependent |
| Members may not know each other | Members are aware of each other's weaknesses |

Figure 3.1

When a staff is team focused, they have a unified vision, and collaborate to help everyone be their best and bring their best! Functioning as a team is only part of it. Your team also needs chemistry to truly be effective. What is team chemistry? In a word, **team chemistry** is all about **productivity**. Teams with good chemistry are more productive because they understand what each member brings to the team and work to maximize strengths and minimize weaknesses of the other **team** members. Additionally, they manage their time better.

**Teachers should have a great support system** of peers/colleagues/administrators. For example, when teachers receive negative specific feedback, they feel isolated. They are not sure who to go to or they may not want others to help because they're embarrassed. That's why it's important to have teams where they feel support and encouragement. It's also important for administrators to know teachers' needs and strengths, so they can provide support or have other teachers provide support. It's great when teams are high achieving, but the members of the team shouldn't be competitive or trying to undermine other team members.

Support builds morale within a team. You'll feel that your work is valued when you contribute to something that produces results. If you offer an idea that helps improve productivity, such as a new online communication system, confidence and trust is built within the team. Each team member has something unique to offer. By working together, members of a team feel a strong sense of belonging and deep commitment to each other and their common goals.

Team members want to work together for the good of the team and understand that combining the skills of numerous people will produce something that could not be created alone. The strengths of each team member are being utilized. As Babe Ruth (2016) said, "The way a team plays as a whole determines its success. You may have the greatest bunch of individual stars in the world, but if they don't play together, the club won't be worth a dime." It is all about chemistry. Here are seven keys to creating team chemistry.

1. **Incorporate team activities**

   Get your staff together and spend a day each month working on team-bonding. This is an important but tricky one because teachers already spend so much time at school and away from their families. Because of this, I would often use a PD day for these types of activities. There is no better way to get to know and appreciate your colleague than to be around them and interact outside of the workplace setting. You may be thinking to yourself, "I'm around my colleagues 24/7 so why do I need to spend even more time with them?" Well, having a stronger connection with your fellow employees will make work more enjoyable and promotes a team mentality. Some examples of team activities include lunch, coffee, or maybe even an activity like bowling.

2. **Create team goals and a mission statement**

   It is important to establish common goals for your team. Create a day at the beginning of the year to sit down with your staff and establish these goals. When you do, split them up into teams of four or five people. First, set goals that are reachable and realistic, but will be difficult to grasp. Then, set goals that you know you will accomplish as a team, ones that are fairly easy. Now, keep all of these goals somewhere safe or post them up to remind everyone of what they're working for. At the end of the year, you can evaluate how well your team has done. The next step is writing a mission statement. Like the first task, each group will come up with their own mission statement and then read them aloud. Then, combine each mission statement to create one that everyone agrees on. Remember to keep it short and concise.

3. **Distribute tasks and responsibility evenly**

   Everyone must work together and contribute in order to be successful as a staff. Therefore, distribute certain tasks and divide responsibility among your staff based upon their strengths. It is important to allow employees, no matter their position, to be able to voice their opinions, give input and even lead certain tasks. Allowing each member to feel vital to the team is essential in improving the school culture. Distributing the workload will also make it easier for each team member. Therefore, the work will be done more quickly and efficiently.

4. **Build trust**

   Trust is the most important variable of teamwork. If you do not trust your staff, then they will not be successful.

In order to build trust, communicate with your staff and be open to their opinions. If a conflict arises, make sure you help to create a solution. Lastly, don't forget the golden rule. If you treat others the way you want to be treated, you will get the same in return. Building trust is the foundation of teamwork and is crucial to the success of the school.

5. **Collaborate**

In education, we need to do a better job of collaborating. We have a false belief that if we seek help, we are incapable or not qualified. Everyone should seek mentoring and/or advice, from the superintendent to the novice teacher. This isn't weakness; this is seeking to be our best! Not an island. One reason for burnout is isolation. Teachers speak an affirmation language, so they need support and encouragement from their team. If we don't value collaboration, then we revert back to working in isolation where teachers tend to compete with each other rather than collaborating.

6. **Make others feel safe to speak up**

Often, leaders intimidate their staff with their title and power when they walk into a room. Successful leaders deflect attention away from themselves and encourage others to voice their opinions. They are experts at making others feel safe to speak-up and confidently share their perspectives and points of view. They use their presence to create an approachable environment.

Teaching is a profession where teachers often feel that their voice is not heard and that their input is not valued. So, it sometimes takes effort to get teachers to speak up. I personally loved teachers who felt comfortable to speak. I knew they trusted me and I knew that they cared enough to say something.

7. **Look for best fit**

I believe using staff's strengths are very important, but sometimes it's as much about the right fit and the right talents. Savvy leaders know that great teams are often built by finding players who embrace their roles—even the roles that aren't always glamorous. Conversely, when leaders look to assemble teams that only include all-stars, they run the risk of poor team chemistry, which can limit results. This is important to remember when you are in the process of hiring new staff and utilizing your current staff.

## Learn Their Stories

General Norman Schwarzkopf once made the statement that,

> I have seen competent leaders who stood in front of a platoon and all they saw was a platoon. But great leaders stand in front of a platoon and see it as forty-four individuals, each of whom has aspirations, each of whom wants to live, each of whom wants to do good.
>
> (Maxwell, 2007)

While you are focused on building a team, remember that they are individuals. One of my most important tasks as an administrator was to learn about my staff. I wasn't satisfied with just name, rank, and serial number. Or in our case, name, grade level, and subject area. As I travel the country now, I can't tell you the number of times that teachers have shared with me that their administration didn't even know their name or what they taught. They felt like they were just an employee and not a person. And most actually felt disrespected because their admin didn't take time to know them.

Remember, effective leadership is not just about hiring the right people, although that is very important. But it's about treating the people you hire the right way. Do you support, encourage, appreciate and connect with them? While your staff may not be your family, you should treat them like family. Family will always go above and beyond for each other.

You may be asking, well, why do I need to know their story?

Remember that teaching is largely a language of affirmation and many teachers speak the language of affirmation.

This means they want to be affirmed not only as a teacher but as a person. There is no better way to affirm someone than to know their story. This shows you value them as a professional and as a person. This helps you better meet their personal and professional needs. Personally, it helps to know when they may be going through something such as sickness, or with a child or parent. Or other life events that can be celebrated. If you know a teacher has a child, or an elderly parent in poor health, then you will be more understanding when issues arise related to family. Just the fact that you ask about family matters can mean the world to a staff member.

From a professional perspective, you may find that a staff member has certain talents or skills that could be utilized. You may find that they desire more leadership opportunities or want to try a new curriculum. They may be working on an advanced degree and may need encouragement, support, or maybe even to leave early. I remember one teacher who was working on her doctorate and she had to drive a long distance once every month or two to attend classes on campus. I would make sure she had her classes covered on the Friday afternoon so she could beat rush hour traffic heading out of town. Even if this meant I had to cover the class. It's these little things that really make a big difference.

**While your staff may not actually be family, make sure you treat them like they are family**. Like family, I made sure that I kept up with their life events as much possible as well. If someone was sick, had a family member pass, or a child received a reward, I tried to either attend or at least acknowledge it with them. I remember a principal messaging me after she had read my book, *Putting Teachers First*. She said she felt guilty because she had not developed strong relationships with her staff and she realized just how much that it affected the school culture. She decided to take out each team of teachers for dinner over a period of several weeks and get to know more about them and their families. This may not be possible if you have a large school, but at least think of ways to learn more about them and build those relationships. We preach relationships, relationships, relationships between the teacher and student, well guess what? It is just as important between administration and the staff.

## Building Unity

A cohesive team promotes an atmosphere that nurtures friendship and loyalty. These close-knit relationships motivate employees to work harder, cooperate, and be supportive of one another. Individuals possess diverse strengths, weaknesses, communication skills, and habits. Therefore, when a teamwork environment is not encouraged this can pose many challenges towards achieving the overall goals and objectives. This creates an environment where employees become focused on promoting their own achievements.

One area that is often not addressed is the competition that exists between some teachers when there isn't a true team concept. Teachers will compete with each other (to have better-looking rooms, to have better lessons/units, to have parents like them more) and it seems to stem from the lack of appreciation they receive from their administration. When teachers don't get that acknowledgement or don't feel valued, they will begin to compete with their peers, subconsciously or not, for that attention. The team concept helps build unity, where teachers realize they aren't in competition with each other, but that they are there to make each other better. Unity creates value for all the members.

However, creating unity is not always easy because teaching has historically been viewed as an isolated profession. Even the teachers' lounge has become more of a place to grab a snack, or check your mail box. It has not been a place to collaborate, or spend time developing relationships; there just simply isn't the time. Because of this mindset, teachers often feel like they are in it alone and when things aren't going well, they don't feel like they have anywhere to turn. However, with cohesive teams, **teachers should have a great support system of peers/colleagues/administrators.**

## Create Vertical Teams

When we think of teams, horizontal ones (such as grade-level teams) usually come to mind. These teams are important because they help teachers focus on best teaching and learning practices. Vertical teams are not as common in most schools, but they are visible in high performing schools.

They require a little more work to create but can be well worth it. The key is to ensure group members bring the right skills to the table and understand their job function. Underperforming teams often don't have the right skills they need to get the job done. Make sure your vertical teams have individuals with varying strengths to bring balance, such as an analytical person, creative person, etc. The teams that know how to work together and divvy up project tasks gain the most from their group's unique mix of knowledge and abilities. You may have some vertical teams in place, such as a leadership or curriculum team, but there are many potential teams that could help you create a high-performing school.

According to an article in *The Balance* by Susan Heathfield (2016), there are five vertical teams that are important to most organizations.

- ◆ **The leadership team** can include all administrators as well as department heads, and others that you feel bring strengths to the team. The leadership team is the group that strategically leads your school.
- ◆ **The motivation or morale team** plans and carries out events and activities that build a positive spirit among employees. The team's responsibilities can include activities such as hosting lunches, planning picnics, fundraising for ill employees, etc.
- ◆ **The safety or environmental team** takes the lead in safety training, monthly safety talks, and the auditing of housekeeping, safety, and workplace organization. Recycling or even "going green" environmental policy recommendations are provided by the team as well.

- ◆ **The culture or communication team** works to define and create the defined company culture necessary for the success of your organization. The team also fosters two-way communication in your organization to ensure employee input up the chain of command. The team may sponsor the monthly newsletter, a weekly company update, quarterly employee satisfaction surveys, and an employee suggestion process.
- ◆ **The teacher wellness team** focuses on health and fitness for employees. Most popular activities include walking clubs, running teams, and periodic testing of health issues such as high blood pressure screenings. This team could set up events, such as a walking challenge to encourage faculty to get moving more. Each participant could be given a pedometer to be downloaded daily at work. At the end of the challenge, there could be prizes for top performers.

## Hire for Strengths

One of my mantras, yes I have many, is that we hire teachers for their strengths, yet we manage them based on their weaknesses. The irony of most hiring is that we seek out candidates who will bring value to the position. We look for people with a strong resume and talents that stand out. However, once we have this perfect candidate in place, the focus becomes more about improving performance or fixing weaknesses than it is about improving the strengths on which they were hired.

I remember my first year of teaching in a very large school system. I was looking forward to bringing my talents and strengths to my new job. However, within the first few weeks of school, I was given something called a PAC, which was a personal appraisal cycle that was meant for me to focus on areas of improvement for the school year. So, I was basically required to spend my first year teaching focusing on two or three areas that I felt needed improvement. This is not a unique situation when you consider that most employees are evaluated with a performance review, which usually focuses on areas of growth, which is just a nice way to say weaknesses.

What strengths does your staff bring? If we think of the staff like a team, then we need people will different talents and skills. For instance, if we were creating a sports team, everyone can't be the quarterback, or the running back, and not everyone can be a receiver. The key to success is to put people in positions where they can be most effective. Then look for other opportunities for them to grow even more, especially if they are seeking out new opportunities.

Finally, we need to hire for strengths and we need to manage for strengths. This means that we don't just evaluate teachers, but we treat them as professionals who are looking to maximize their strengths and potential. I suggest instead of the traditional evaluation or an end of the year evaluation that you include aspirational conversations. These conversations help you under-stand the goals and needs of each staff member to really help them be the best teammate possible.

There are five key questions to ask staff on a regular basis, in place of the event, such as employee review (a review ultim-ately focused on what they need to work on, or a focused set of questions regarding employee improvement). In education, this suggests formative assessment (ongoing, interim) in place of summative assessment (the test, the autopsy to determine if one passed or failed). These five questions become more productive.

### Aspirational Conversation
1) Have we helped you succeed?
2) What do you think we do well? Such as reading, extra-curricular, etc.
3) What do you see, such as in other schools, that would make us do better?
4) What would make you want to leave us?
5) What are your professional goals? How can we help you achieve them?

People often leave because they're not valued and because there is no room to grow. Does one desire to work towards an administrative role? Or maybe take on different role in the school? Tell them you will help them get there. Value them by letting them know that if they will be the best teacher they can be every day for you, then you will help them achieve their goals.

## Develop a Team of Leaders

Because of the high turnover of principals, there is a propensity to feel like you need to have a say in every decision and micro manage others, because the buck does stop with you after all. But maybe one of the reasons we have high turnover and burn out of principals and administrators is because we continue this vicious cycle of expecting them to turn around a school, increase test scores, or raise morale all by themselves. This is more like a recipe for disaster than it is a dynamic school culture.

Even when some administrators are willing to give opportunities to lead, they expect teachers to do it just like they would. When this happens, the administrator may unwittingly end up micromanaging the teachers to make sure it is "done how they would do it." I remember a specific incidence between a principal and an assistant principal in my first year of teaching. The principal wanted the assistant principal to write an article for the local newspaper. The assistant principal spent a few days working on it and was going to send it in to the paper, but the principal asked to read over it first. The next day, the assistant principal got the paper back and it was covered in red pen marks and notes. The principal had rewritten the whole article to sound like she wanted it to sound. The AP said she felt like she was a student back in high school instead of a school leader.

Give team members actual responsibility/authority on teams or in delegating work to them. In fact, **the mark of effective leaders is their ability to develop and empower their followers**. Employees, after all, are the greatest asset an organization possesses and this includes schools. But, as we learned earlier, many leaders work within a transactional (rewards vs.

punishment) style of leadership, so the talents of employees are not fully utilized. Interestingly, Gallup research shows that people who feel like their strengths are utilized in their job are six times more likely to be engaged at work and three times more likely to feel like they have a high quality of life. However, the same research shows that two-thirds of workers *don't* feel like their strengths are being fully utilized. This means they don't feel engaged at work, have lower productivity, and don't feel like they have a high quality of life.

Now imagine if two-thirds or more of employees felt like their strengths were being utilized. Imagine the level of engagement and productivity that would exist. If this were a faculty of teachers, imagine how the students would respond to such an environment. It would impact the entire school community. Adults aren't different from children when it comes to motivation. If we only focus on areas of weakness, or needs improvement, then people will never be intrinsically motivated! However, when you focus on people's talents and strengths, then they can't help but be motivated. In fact, People are nearly 100 percent actively engaged in their jobs when their administration/leaders focus upon their strengths. According to Gallup (Lopez, 2013), About seven in ten teachers are "not engaged" or "actively disengaged" in their work, meaning they are emotionally disconnected from their work environment. Thirty-one percent are engaged. As teacher engagement is the number 1 predictor and driver of student engagement, these findings have serious implications for students and administrators.

People often leave because there is no room to grow. Ask them what their personal vision is. Do they want to be in administration or have they ever even thought about it? Do they want any other leadership roles? Do they want to grow in other ways professionally, like becoming published? Then tell them you will help them get there. For example, let them know that if they will be the best teacher they can be every day for you, then you will help them achieve their goals.

Leadership is about giving ownership to the employee of their personal productivity and self-improvement. Provide the tools, provide the training, assign work/projects according to strengths, set the minimum standards, set the stretch goals mutu- ally, give feedback and coaching, and provide ongoing resources for their personal access and improvement. The "resources" may include tutorials, a peer mentor, or more training. Effective leaders make sure all these steps and processes are in place—and then expect productivity as part of the "ownership" arrangement. **However, don't expect them to do it the same way you would do it. Otherwise, you will become a micromanager and they won't be effective**.

**Share leadership vision**. Help people feel that they are part of something bigger than themselves and their individual job. Do this by making sure they know, and have access to, the organization's overall mission, vision, and strategic plans.

**Strengthen your staff's competence and confidence**. Try the following simple exercise. Before every interaction—whether it's a one-minute, one-on-one conversation or a one-hour group meeting—ask yourself this question: What can I do in this inter- action so that this person feels more confident, capable, and self- determined than before this interaction started? If you then act on your answers, you'll be continuously developing and motiv- ating others.

1. **Delegate early**
   Make an effort to delegate the task early to avoid unneces- sary pressure. This allows the person to better plan the task. It also gives them time to make adjustments if needed.
2. **Select the right person**
   Ensure that the person has the time to take on the respon- sibility. Assess the skills and capabilities of your staff and assign the task to the most appropriate person. Make sure the person has the training and resources to succeed. It should not always be just about who will volunteer, so offer incentives if at all possible.
3. **Communicate the rationale and benefit**
   Identify the reason for the task and how it will contribute to the goals of the school or team. Also, point out how the delegated task could benefit the person. For example,

develop a specific skill. that is needed to get promoted. Remember a routine task to you may be a new challenging task to a staff member.

4. **Delegate the entire task to one person**
This gives the person the responsibility, increases their motivation, and avoids ambiguity in accountability. Otherwise, different people will have different ideas about who does what when. This will also keep you from micromanaging the person while performing the task.

5. **Set clear goals and expectations**
Be clear and specific on what is expected. Give information on what, why, when, who, and where. You might leave the "how" to them. Be prepared to accept input from subordinates. Confirm and verify task goals and expectations.

6. **Delegate responsibility and authority**
Ensure that the subordinate is given the relevant responsibility and authority to complete the task. Let the subordinate complete the task in the manner they choose, as long as the results are what you specified. Be willing to accept ideas from the subordinate on task fulfillment.

7. **Provide support, guidance, and instructions**
Point subordinates to the resources they may need to complete the task or project. That could be people they need to coordinate with, crucial information, or being willing to be a resource yourself.

8. **Take personal interest in the progress of delegated task**
Request to be updated on the progress of the task, provide assistance when necessary. Be careful not to be intrusive or you may give the perception that you do not trust them. Keep communication lines open; regular meetings on large tasks can provide this ongoing feedback.

9. **If you're not satisfied with the progress, don't take the project back immediately**
Rather, continue to work with them and ensure they understand the project to be their responsibility. Give advice on ways to improve. This ensures accountability and dependability.

10. **Evaluate and recognize performance**

Evaluate results more than methods. Analyze cause of insufficient performance for improvements and recognize successes as soon as possible.

There is nothing that can boost the confidence of your staff and make them feel empowered than to allow them opportunities to contribute to the success of your vision. Influencing your team is the most important aspect of your job because it is where you have the potential for the greatest impact. When your team feels like you trust, respect, support, and appreciate them, there's not much they wouldn't do to help you succeed.

# 4

# Influencing Communication

Communication is possibly the most important trait of leadership, yet it is often taken for granted. I think it's overlooked because it's like walking, we learn to talk at an early age, so we think we are efficient at it, since we have done it for so long. But how effective are we really at communicating? Effective communication and effective leadership are closely intertwined. As an administrator, you need to be a skilled communicator in countless relationships with staff, students, parents, and community at large. Effective communication with faculty members is important for technical performance, as well as for maintaining morale within the school. So, this chapter will, as the theme of the book suggests, focus on **influencing communication**.

Effective communication as a leader is essential. I have been told throughout my career that I am an effective communicator. I can tell you that the secret to my success really boils down to two key points.

1. I am a good listener. When speaking with staff or people in general, I spend most of the time intently listening to them with my full attention. I actually don't do a lot of talking, but really listen to what they're saying, not saying, and how they are saying it.

2. I speak as simplistically as possible. I heard a minister say many years ago that you put the cookies on the bottom shelf so everyone can reach them. I remembered that when I took on my first administrator position and I especially keep it in mind when I am speaking in public. If no one understands what you're saying, communication has not occurred.

I guess the cookie analogy really connected with me in the second key point because it is focused on food! But it's true. Whether we are talking to staff, parents, students, or the community, **simplicity is also the soul of wit**. This means to never use educational jargon or those $20 buzzwords that pop up every few weeks in education.

Therefore, as we focus on communication in this chapter, remember it is not so much about the technical aspects of communication, but it is all about influence. If you have created a positive culture of influence then you can communicate your/team's vision, goals, and objectives and have commitment and buy-in from your staff. Success is really about commitment. While I try not to focus on negatives, please don't try to communicate and rule from a place of compliance. So, as a leader, stay away from using these phrases:

1. It's about the kids, not you.
2. Because I'm in charge, or, I said so.
3. It's how we do it, or, always been done.
4. It's what you signed up for.

And not, just these phrases, but any that make it appear that the only reason to listen and follow is because you are in the position of authority. Former British Prime Minister, Margaret Thatcher said it best when she stated, "Being a leader is like being a lady. If you have to remind people you are, you aren't." If you have built a strong positive culture, then your staff will follow because they are committed to your leadership, not because you are the boss. As you are about to see, **communication is not about control but connection!**

## Communicate to Connect

If there is one area that leaders can improve, I believe it is communication. Most people think being a great leader is about being the smartest person in the room, but it isn't. Effective leadership is about connecting with others and creating a sense of confidence and camaraderie with staff members. None of this happens without exceptional communication skills, which involves more than simply talking.

As mentioned before, we don't think about it because we talk, and communicate daily. However, do you feel like you are a strong communicator in public, especially in front of large crowds? Most people are nervous in front of audiences, and educators don't have a special vaccination for this phobia. When you aren't comfortable, it makes it much harder to connect. And effective leaders understand that communication is really about connecting.

I remember meeting with a principal several years ago, who began his career as a scientist and even worked for NASA for several years. He made education a second career and eventually became an administrator. He said he felt disconnected from his staff and didn't feel like they were ever on the same page. Even though he was successful and in a leadership role, he was not an effective principal mainly because he couldn't communicate well. In fact, even though he had a brilliant mind, he had a rocky time as a principal because he simply couldn't connect well with his staff. I shared some of the strategies with him as he prepared to search for another position that I will share in this section and hopefully these strategies will benefit you as well.

I have interviewed many superintendents over the years and asked them what is the main issue that they see in poor leaders. The answer is usually relationships, but when I dig a little deeper into their responses, it usually has more to do with the ability to communicate and connect to build on those relationships. So how does someone use communication to connect? These are my top ten key ways to connect with communication.

1. **Communicate early and often**. It's one of your single most important roles as a leader. Don't be a leader that has to be found. Always be available and always be communicating with your staff. Start everyday communicating over the loud speaker. This lets everyone know you are there, and on the ball. This actually gives a sense of security to the staff, and especially students.

2. **Verbal connection**. Our words have a powerful impact and people respond to the words we use and the tone of our voice. People can recognize emotions from the way you speak. The way you deliver your message can either drive people away or draw them in. If you want to connect with people, be mindful of your choice of words and the manner by which you deliver them. Often just slowing down and letting your words sink in will increase the impact of your message.

3. **Visual connection**. Before you even open your mouth to speak, people have already formed a visual impression of you. How you look, dress, and behave are all factors to how they will accept what you have to say. Give them a visual of someone uninterested, disconnected, or distracted, and you'll quickly lose that connection. What people see us do can far outweigh any words we actually say. Make sure you clear your agenda before entering critical conversations with staff or parents.

4. **Share your thoughts and feelings**. This is very difficult for some people. But if you really want to connect with others, you must be willing to share what is going on with you. Sharing how you are thinking and feeling will help the other person in the conversation to be more open to sharing as well. Sharing and listening to one another creates connections and understanding of each other.

5. **Be open minded**. If you expect to improve any personal or professional relationship, you have to be willing to hear what others are thinking, whatever that may be. If you hear something that you didn't expect, don't be unsettled by the message. Ask questions and for examples to understand the other person's perspective without defending

yourself. Seek first to understand and then thank the person for sharing their perspective. Don't get defensive in a conversation. Remember the tough conversations are about ideas, not individuals.

6. **Be empathetic.** This is not easy if you have not been trained to put yourself in another person's shoes. One simple way to increase your ability to empathize with others is to ask yourself this question: "What would this person have to think and feel in order to say or do that?" This question requires you to relinquish your perspective for a moment and observe the other person's world or experience from their perspective. Remember that what we deem to be irrational is rational to someone else. The challenge is to understand the rationality behind the feelings, words, and actions that we don't understand.

7. **Be brief and to the point.** I always say that when it comes to communication, it is quality over quantity. In order to get the public's attention and keep it, you must be brief and to the point. Parents can't digest lengthy newsletters. They need short articles with more graphics. One sheet of paper is best. Use approximately 6th-grade reading level. Most parents will spend less than a minute reading what you send home. Also, never use educational jargon. PS: Just say "no" to acronyms! Most people don't know what they stand for anyway. When I hear words like "fidelity" and "rigor", even my mind starts to wander.

8. **Be a good storyteller**, or work to improve on this area. There is no better way to connect than with stories. Think of how people relate: it's through stories. Don't think it's true? Look at any conversation on Twitter for example, and you will see people agree or disagree, not based upon theory or research, but on their own anecdotal experiences. Trust me, I experience this on a daily basis on social media! Our experiences, our stories, are our reality. **Stories** are a great way to communicate ideas. That's how we are wired. We like neat theories and tidy spreadsheets, but we soon forget them. We don't forget

stories, we are drawn to them, we connect with them. Stories of identity and purpose help build the team concept. Stories also elicit emotions and there is no more powerful motivator than our emotions. When you stir the emotions of those you lead, there's no limit to what they will do for you!

9. **Honesty is the backbone of relationships**. Remember, you can speak truth without being too critical and that's where empathy comes in. Things can be said in a gentle way.

   Great leaders communicate trust in their faculty to handle situations appropriately. How? They tell them the truth, even if it's bad news. Great leaders explain their reasoning behind decisions. They listen well and gather input before deciding. They listen more than they speak. They guide with great questions to help faculty members develop their own solutions to problems instead of telling them what to do. They express their trust and confidence in faculty to do a great job and take the appropriate action.

10. **Listening**. Leaders have to be approachable to get the one thing they need most to do their job, which is **feedback**. Leaders will not be successful for long without feedback from those who serve their "customers"—students, parents, and the community at large. When leaders see themselves as intellectually "above it all," they cut themselves off from communication from the frontline. That is deadly.

    Also ask for input from your staff. I have never understood leaders who tell staff what to do without ever seeking their input, since they are the experts who will be implementing it. Listening is hailed as the Holy Grail of interpersonal communication, and for good reason: without it, communication becomes very difficult. And you don't want to just listen; you want to empathetically listen. You don't want to be that person who talks and talks but doesn't listen to anything the other person says. It's a good way to have no friends or noncommitted staff.

## Communicate Transparency

In the previous section, I mentioned communicating early and often. This doesn't mean you need meetings all the time, but what it means is that you should always be willing to share any information pertinent to the staff.

In the past, especially before the technology explosion, knowledge was power. For centuries, we have all known that knowledge is power. The basic management hierarchy of almost all organizations is based on this premise. The top person in any company knows the vision, they share that down, and so forth. Along these lines, knowledge becomes very powerful.

Your boss knows about something, a big change that will take place next month, but she can't share it with you, just yet. You want that information. You want to know how it will affect your job, your life, the organization, your co-workers, etc.

Your boss' boss knows a little more, your boss wants to know what they know. This is how most organizational leadership still runs on a daily basis. They squeeze every drop of power out of the knowledge they held.

Most information doesn't need to be on a need to know basis. And in many cases, when leaders hold "their cards close to the vest", then it's usually to make themselves feel more important or powerful.

However, effective leaders find it more beneficial to pass along knowledge quickly so their teams can use that knowledge to help the school be more successful. In the information age, the world of knowledge is moving very fast. If you sit on knowledge for a moment, it could end up being useless because someone else will beat you to the punch.

Jason Jennings, bestselling author and speaker, shared with me in an interview of the time he spent with the Koch Brothers gathering information for his research. At the end of their visit, Charles Koch told him that he could take a copy of their five-year strategic plan to look over for any information that he needed.

Jason asked, "don't you want me to sign a non-disclosure?" Charles replied, "No, in fact we send a copy of this out to our competitors to let them know how and when they are going to die." He was joking of course, but his point was that it's not the knowledge that makes them successful, but that it is the execution of it.

Charles went on to tell him that he felt sorry for Jason because he was so old. And Jason replied, "What do you mean? I am not even as old as you," Charles said, "only old people believe that knowledge is power. Once, knowledge was power, when not everyone had access to it. But everyone has access to it now, so there is no need to try and keep it from everyone. Especially within an organization."

Charles said,

> it is not knowledge that is power now, but that flawless execution is power now. And the more people in your organization that have the knowledge or are "In the know," the more likely you are to have flawless execution, because everyone is on the same page.

Jason said he was interviewing the Smuckers brothers and asked them if he needed to sign a non-disclosure? Tim Smucker replied, "What type of people do you hang out with?" He said, "No, you don't need to sign anything. In fact, we have our strategic plan available to anyone who wants to see it." This reinforced the idea to Jason that it's not knowledge that is power anymore, but it is how the power is used, flawless execution!

Jason went on to share that he believes in today's culture that knowledge kept in secrecy, or the holding on to knowledge, is the currency of the unproductive. These are the people who only have value because of the secrets they know. They are unproductive, they do very little, but people are afraid of them because they know all the secrets. You may have experienced a situation with a teacher or teachers who fit this description. You wonder how they keep their job because they seem so negative and don't do a great job in the classroom, but they seem to know all the gossip and confidential information that the rest of the staff is not privy too. I remember a teacher like this and she let everyone know that they better not get on her bad side. People often joked that she must have the goods on the administration. There were times when she seemed to almost antagonize some teachers and administrators. It was a very toxic culture, created in part because the principal felt like holding on to knowledge was power.

These leaders may keep secrets because it gives them a sense of self-importance, or they are afraid the competition will know what they are up to. But great leaders understand that it's not knowledge, but execution of knowledge that is what makes organizations successful. So be willing to share as much information as you can so that the grapevine doesn't thrive and so everyone functions as a team, not as competitors.

When leadership is transparent, it diminishes the negativity of the grapevine. There are no secrets, surprises, or just a few people in the know. Everyone is on same page working together. That interaction fuels action because the more people share information, the more they learn; and the more they learn, the more they identify opportunities to address existing problems, challenges, or opportunities.

As a leader, rather than trying to hoard something that can be easily acquired, I shared my knowledge. Two people will collectively know more than one. Three will know more than two. And when you have a room full of smart people sharing their knowledge, there's very little you can't accomplish together. The flawless execution of knowledge is powerful.

## Listen to Connect

The most important and most overlooked aspect of communication is listening. I remember hearing Larry King say years ago that, "I remind myself every morning: Nothing I say this day will teach me anything. So, if I'm going to learn, I must do it by listening."

If there is one area that I think most leaders can improve, it is in listening to their staff. Gallup polls showed that teachers are the profession who feel like their voice is heard the least and that their input is all but ignored. This seems to be common in education. The problem with this is that you have teachers who very likely have more experience and expertise than you do. They shouldn't be seen as a threat, but you should listen to their input.

Taking the time for in-depth conversations with teachers, other administrators and student leaders should be the first order of business. Most importantly, this effort should not be wasted on superficial exchanges, in which little of substance gets heard and said, or by giving license to grievance airing. *How* a leader listens will establish the tone going forward as well as providing the leader with invaluable insights into what can and should be done.

Have you ever had a conversation with someone where you said very little but at the end, she told you how much she enjoyed the conversation? This is because you took the time to listen. One of the most effective communication skills is listening. Remember that communication is about connecting, and you can't connect if you don't listen to your teachers. The difficulty with being a good listener is that it makes us focus on others, and by nature we tend to be focused on ourselves. But the beauty of listening is that your teachers, the experts, have feedback, ideas, and suggestions that they would like to share with you. One of the best ways to show them they are important is to listen. Listening to understand and relate is a mindset—not just a skillset.

In today's world of social media, we tend to have more distractions, and those distractions interfere with our ability to focus and listen. But the selfless leader wants to not only listen to their staff but really connect with them. To serve is dependent upon our ability to listen and perceive the needs of others. We serve by creating a space where individual voices can be heard and validated. Here are a few listening strategies to try the next time you're conversing with teachers.

♦ *Listen to relate, not respond.* Usually when we communicate with others, we are more interested in our own thoughts, feelings, and viewpoints. Even when we are actively engaged in a conversation, it is more about waiting to give our response than about relating to what they are saying. Stephen Covey, author of *The 7 Habits of Highly Successful People*, once said, "Most people do not listen with the intent to understand; they listen with the intent to reply" (2004). To really connect, we have to focus more on listening to relate. That means understanding what the speaker is trying to convey, the emotions being expressed, and what the person is hoping to achieve through the conversation. In essence, it is about them! The following are a few ways to move from listening to respond to listening to relate and understand.

◆ *Get rid of outside distractions.* How many times have you been interrupted in a conversation by a phone dinging, ringing, or binging? It is impossible to focus, much less truly relate, if your attention is distracted. Put everything down and shut off all technology. Relax, get comfortable, and focus.

◆ *Don't interrupt*. Have you ever had someone try to talk over you? It can be quite frustrating. Until the person has finished speaking, don't talk—even if they say something that causes a reaction in you and you're tempted to interrupt. You can always go back to a point and respond later.

◆ *Keep an open mind*. Don't judge what they say, just listen. You will have time to process the information and you will get an opportunity to respond. But remember the key is to relate, so keep an open mind to their ideas. They may present valid points that you may not hear if you are busy thinking of your response.

◆ *Use attentive cues.* Look the speaker in the eyes. Lean in to show attentiveness. Also, pay attention to the speaker's nonverbal cues. Does their body language and other cues match their words? If it does not match up then you know the non-verbal cues are speaking the truth. If it does match up then it indicates trust, honesty, and other details.

## Challenge the Process, Don't Accept the Status Quo

During World War II, researchers at the Center for Naval Analysis faced a critical problem. Many bombers were getting shot down on runs over Germany. The naval researchers knew they needed hard data to solve this problem and went to work. After each mission, the bullet holes and damage from each bomber was painstakingly reviewed and recorded. The researchers poured over the data looking for vulnerabilities.

The data began to show a clear pattern with most damage to the wings and body of the plane. The solution to their problem was clear. Increase the armor on the plane's wings and body. But there was a problem. The analysis was completely wrong.

Before the planes were modified, a Hungarian-Jewish statistician named Abraham Wald reviewed the data. Wald had fled Nazi-occupied Austria and worked in New York with other academics to help the war effort.

Wald's review pointed out a critical flaw in the analysis. The researchers had only looked at bombers who'd returned to base. Missing from the data? Every plane that had been shot down.

But the research wasn't a wasted effort. These surviving bombers rarely had damage in the cockpit, engine, and parts of the tail. This wasn't because of superior protection to those areas. In fact, these were the most vulnerable areas on the entire plane.

The researchers' bullet hole data had created a map of the exact places that the bomber could be shot and still survive. With the new analysis in hand, crews reinforced the bombers' cockpit, engines, and tail armor. The result was fewer fatalities and greater success of bombing missions. This analysis proved to be so useful that it continued to influence military plane design up through the Vietnam war.

What if Abraham Wald had not spoken up and challenged the process? What if he just went along with the crowd? It may have greatly changed the air success in the war. I have long said that some administrators don't like strong teachers because they may see them as a threat. The reality is that these strong teachers often bring a lot to the table and they care about their students. They want what is best for the students and will speak out against the status quo if there is a better way. Don't fear these teachers but embrace them.

Now, I am not talking about teachers who are just argumentative, try to divide the team or are not productive. That's a different situation that needs to be addressed with the individual, but challenging the process actually shows that you have a healthy team culture, where people feel free to speak up and discuss alternatives.

### There's a Huge Difference between Complaining and Challenging the Process

Know the difference and how to respond accordingly. One is negative and one can be very positive. However, if your best teachers are complaining, you might better take a step back and figure out why. Remember don't take challenging the process as a personal attack, but be open to different perspectives and new ways of thinking. You have a staff of very educated and experienced professionals, so utilize their talents and strengths and be confident enough in your own leadership for ideas and strategies to be challenged. Here are a few points to remember when the process is challenged.

- ◆ Give in. Allow others to challenge your ideas. Adapt your thoughts. Problems have more than one solution. Leaders who can't adapt end up ineffective and going it alone.
- ◆ Stay focused. Challenges feel personal because you're challenging someone's good idea. Keep the goal in mind. Unfocused challenges feel like personal attacks.
- ◆ Expect resistance. Don't take opposition personally. Committed team members are seeking the best methods.
- ◆ Expose rather than hide. Speak clearly and candidly about intentions, assumptions, and objectives. Manipulation produces resistance.
- ◆ Remain optimistic about others. Believe teammates seek what's best, even when they disagree.

# Connecting through Conflict

I have been fortunate to interview, meet, and even befriend leaders from all different fields. Over the years, I have found that there are a few common traits among the most successful leaders. One of those traits is that they are good at handling conflict and confrontation. This doesn't mean that they enjoy it or seek it out, but that they have developed the skills to handle it in a positive light.

Conflict is often seen as negative. But conflict is really a natural part of relationships and the key is not to avoid them, but to handle them properly. When leaders understand how to influence conflict, and confrontation, then there is very little they can't handle.

These **tough conversations can nurture deep professional learning as individuals and teams explore new ideas for practice, as well as actual strengthen relationships among the team**. However, they may also lead to conflict, especially when you have individuals with different strengths, perspectives, and experiences. Conflict however, is not necessarily bad, as discussed in the communication chapter. In fact, team conflict can sometimes create better solutions. Of course, we don't want people who have to argue with every idea just for the sake of argument, but if something doesn't seem as logical as it sounds, maybe there does need to be more discussion.

## Team Conflict Can Actually Lead to Better Practices or Improved Results

This concept is worth repeating because conflict is often seen as a negative and divisive to teams. But the reality is you have people on your teams with different strengths, perspectives, and expertise, so some may identify issues that others don't see or there may simply be disagreements.

I think of conflict as being kind of like stress. It's not that we will never encounter it, but it is how we deal with it that matters. While confronting someone is not really pleasant, it's something you must do as a leader, and how you do it makes all the difference. I think it is one of the reasons that I have been so successful in my career is that I learned early on how to deal with confrontation. In fact, this is one of my favorite topics to speak on because understanding how to deal with confrontation will make every leaders life so much easier, not just professionally but personally as well.

One person I have had many conversations with on the topic of conflict is Dianna Booher, a communication expert and author of *Speak with Confidence*. She says that leaders must believe that confrontation can be a positive situation. After all, confrontation handled well has many benefits:

- ◆ Innovative solutions to problems
- ◆ Improvements to the status quo
- ◆ Stronger confidence in implementing ideas
- ◆ Stronger relationships
- ◆ Greater harmony
- ◆ Improved communication
- ◆ Better teamwork
- ◆ Greater understanding
- ◆ Increased engagement on the job
- ◆ Strong passion and commitment to see success of the ideas developed

So, don't shy away from conflict when it arises, but rather use the opportunity to build stronger relationships with your staff. The reason confrontation is hard is that it is outside our comfort zone. Since no one really likes confrontation, the problem is we tend to wait until we can't take it anymore to confront someone. We let things build until emotions are high, and then we tend to overreact. At this point we aren't thinking rationally and not really looking to compromise or resolve the issue. **An effective leader can actually use conflict constructively to influence positive growth among their staff.** Here are what I consider the key strategies to help you deal with confrontation and actually make it a beneficial part of the communication process:

1.  *Focus on being proactive, not reactive*

Imagine that you have a teacher who is consistently late. Ok, some of you don't have to imagine because you have a teacher who is excessively late. Do you react by sending out a mass email stating that all teachers must arrive on time? When you address it in this manner, the odds of the person correcting their behavior is slim. More than likely, you are going to hurt the morale of the whole staff, because good teachers will remember that one time in a snowstorm that they were two minutes late. And they will dwell on this negativity the rest of the day, or maybe even week. And the teacher who is late? Well he won't give it another thought, because you didn't address him specifically, so he assumes your talking about someone else. Never be reactive to this type of situation. Reactive is when you let your emotions control the situation. Being proactive means that you let your sound judgement take control of the situation.

When posed with this scenario, Dianna Booher (2017, personal communication), Communication Expert and bestselling author, shared the following with me in an interview:

> Leaders will do well to learn to give direct, straight-forward feedback to individuals. In general, praise in public; coach on negative situations in private. Take the example of teachers who frequently arrive late. If 99 per-cent of your staff arrive on time throughout the year, you might want to send a mass email to thank them for their continually commitment to punctuality, say how much your appreciate this because it sets a good example for students, and ensures that they are prepared for the day. Then for the few who are routinely tardy, have coaching conversations with them individually. Ask their reasons for their routine tardiness. Is it that they have a first-period planning and don't feel like they need to arrive at regular time? Do they drop off an elderly parent for therapy at a local nursing home? Do they just not get up in time to get to work? Again, state the expectation,

discover if they have an excuse or a real reason for their tardiness. If you're dealing with a reason, brainstorm for creative solutions. Restate the expectation and get their agreement to meet that expectation. Let them know what next steps might be if they fail to meet the agreed-upon standard. Most likely, if they have a reason (versus an excuse), you will have agreed upon a creative solution and the "next steps" part of the conversation may be unnecessary.

As Dianna suggests, there may be times when tough conversations have to occur, and next steps may be needed to correct the issue. Just make sure it is not something that affects the entire staff. Be proactive in praising good behavior, and be proactive in getting ahead of major issues by confronting the person individually.

2. *Focus on relating, not on being right*

When we let issues stew, we let our emotions take control. It becomes no longer about the issue, but about being right. Even in the midst of communicating, each person is not really listening to each other, but waiting for a turn to speak, or interrupting to make a point. Try to remember that it's not about being right, it's about relating.

In fact, when you as the administrator begin these tough conversations, your goal should not be to win the argument, but to relate and come to some kind of solution. There is a reason they're called RELATION-ships and not RIGHT-ships. You have to be willing to relate to the person, even if that person is wrong. One important point for leaders to remember is that if you have to use your position of power to win an argument, then you really haven't won. You could be seen as a bully and not as someone who is willing to compromise and resolve issues. Some may think that the topic of bullying is not important, but in a recent survey of medium-sized school districts, 25 percent of employees reported that they had been bullied (Long, 2012).

Yes, 25 percent of teachers felt their administrators had bullied them. A key method to removing this perception is in handling conflicts better and focusing on relating rather than being right.

3. *Focus on the issue, not on the individual*

When conflict arises, it could be more about the personalities of the individuals than about the actual issues. You have to distinguish between the two. For instance, weak leaders don't necessarily like strong teachers because they see them as a threat. So, conflict may arise when these teachers inevitably speak their mind on a topic. But when dealing with the issue, rather than individual, what we are saying is that you should focus on the behavior at the root of the conflict and not on the personality of the individuals. If Jim is always late for school, is Jim lazy? Or does Jim lack time management skills? One is a focus on the individual; one is a focus on his behavior.

When focusing on the issue, there is no real solution if we take the perspective that Jim is lazy. In fact, challenging the person and not the behavior will make them defensive and make the situation more difficult. But if we look at the behavior, then we can find solutions to correct behavior. Challenging the behavior and not the person allows for a shared review of the behavior that caused the issues or concern, and there is less likelihood of defensiveness in the person whose behavior is challenged.

4. *Focus on the future, not on the conflict*

One of two things results from conflict. Either there is some sort of compromise and a solution to the issue, or maybe there is no resolution and there has to be the "next steps" conversation. Hopefully you reach a compromise more often than not. However, if there needs to be a next step, then that has to be addressed without a personality conflict. Make sure your teachers know that it is not personal and that correcting a problem or issue is all that matters to you.

As you can see, conflict or confrontation doesn't need to be avoided, but it does require removing emotions as much as possible and focusing on the issues. While it is human nature to react to situations emotionally, if you follow the steps and strategies that we have just discussed, you can have positive outcomes, even from the most tense of situations.

When conflict is seen as potentially improving the status quo, or creating healthier relationships, then how can it be viewed as anything but positive? Not to mention, leaders who know how to handle confrontation are more likely to deal with issues individually and less likely to make sweeping generalizations that lower morale of the whole staff. So, don't avoid confrontation, but utilize it appropriately as an *effective* leader.

# 5

# Influencing Morale

The following is an excerpt from the USO archives (Oldenburg, 2016). The tiny island of Diego Garcia, in the middle of the Indian Ocean. Christmas 1972. Seabee Ron Ronning, 19, and his fellow naval construction buddies worked around the clock to build a runway for Bob Hope's C-141. The comedy legend was about to put on what would be his final USO show of the Vietnam War.

It was 1 p.m., and it was hot. "On that island it was 113 degrees every day," said Ronning, now 63 and a former mayor of Appleton, Minnesota. That Christmas Day, "It was raining, pouring rain before the show. Then, all of a sudden, the sunlight came out."

Men hung from cranes and other heavy equipment for a better view of the stage. Hope, twirling his golf club and delivering one-liners, was a huge hit. "He got a standing ovation from the minute he came on," Ronning said.

Comedian Redd Foxx, singer Lola Falana, and a dozen "American Beauties," among others, joined Hope on that tour. But Hope and his USO gang's presence on the tiny island was about much more than entertainment.

"They increased the morale immensely," Ronning recalled. "It was miserable there. But that visit really made the difference in our deployment—that got us through the next four, five months. He brought such enthusiasm, brought your life back to you. You felt like you were renewed," he said. "That was one of the biggest thrills of my life."

It's a scene that played out again and again for nearly 50 years—from World War II, through Vietnam, to the Gulf War. The legendary comedian traveled the world, visiting remote outposts in Alaska, dangerous battle zones in Beirut and isolated battleships in faraway seas to put on USO shows. Bob Hope was world renowned as an actor and comedian, but to the USO and our military, he was known for half a century as The One Man Morale Machine!

As a leader, one of your main goals should be to rally your troops, to be a one man or one woman morale machine! Having a good curriculum and latest technology is wonderful, but there is nothing that affects the classroom more than a teacher who is motivated, supported, and appreciated. I know I would personally interact with as many of my staff every day to check in on them, but to also gauge the climate of the school. Were people mainly happy or was there underlying issues that I could pick up on?

As an administrator, you have little control over more pay or resources. However, you do have control over things like jeans day, providing coffee or lunch for your staff, covering duties or even classes. These may seem like little things to you, but they can do wonders for staff morale and appreciation and let them know you.

## Increasing Rapport

While leadership is more than morale and rapport, those aspects really are the cornerstones of effective leadership. And when you consider the reasons for building rapport, it just makes sense. Some of the most quoted statistics from Gallup poll (www.gallup. com/services/182138/state-american-manager.aspx) show:

- ◆ Only **30 percent of employees** are engaged at work.
- ◆ The *manager accounts for* **at least 70 percent** of the variance in employee engagement.

- Only **35 percent of managers** are engaged.
- **50 percent** of Americans have left a job to *"get away from their manager at some point in their career."*

The poll also revealed that people who use their strengths every day and who feel valued are:

- Three times more likely to report having an excellent quality of life,
- Six times more likely to be engaged at work,
- 8 percent more productive and
- 15 percent less likely to quit their jobs.

Can you imagine what leaders would be willing to do to get their staff to be six times more engaged at work? Yet, all you need to do is help them be their best self, support, and value them. That is the secret to building a strong positive team culture. As you build rapport with your team, they will be more receptive to your feedback, motivated to bring their best, more loyal to your leadership, and everyone will enjoy work more.

So how do we begin to build this rapport?

## Praise Job Performance

Stronger relationships develop when principals take time to notice teachers' efforts and accomplishments. Everyone needs and wants praise, even those who state differently. A study completed by Blasé and Blasé (1999) found that praise focusing on specific and concrete teaching behaviors significantly affected teacher motivation, self-esteem, and efficacy. It also fostered teacher reflective behavior, including reinforcement of effective teaching strategies, risk taking and innovative/creativity.

## Using Teachers'/Staff Ideas

Building on the previous point, whenever it is possible to use a suggestion or idea presented by a teacher, use it! Or at least look into the possibility of using it, even if it has to be fine-tuned. This not only helps keep that teacher motivated, it may encourage other teachers to offer their suggestions or ideas, too. Just be sure to give credit to the person who originally came up with the idea, as failing to do so could have the opposite effect on staff members.

## Be Confident and Friendly

People are naturally attracted to warm, bubbly people so make sure you are friendly. Not only will it make you more likeable, you will also help those who are nervous to feel more relaxed around you. Everyone prefers being around people who are pleasant. One of the principal's primary responsibilities is to establish and maintain a positive work environment. While you can't be held responsible for other adults' behaviors, you can set the expectations and model behaviors that promote a positive climate for all staff, students, and parents. This may seem like it doesn't need to be said, but I can't tell you the number of teachers who tell me their administration doesn't even say hello in the hallway, or worse, who doesn't even know their name. I have often said **be one of the reasons that a teacher wants to stay at your school, but at the very least don't be a reason they want to leave.**

## Squad Goals

When a group of people create a set of agreed values, and understand which behaviors support those values, then all rules reduce to one; live the values. Devoting time as a new leader to establishing a team's values not only builds great relationships between you and the team, but everyone else as well. It's a highly effective way to cement a team when the individuals agree upon the values, providing a common bond between all members. And remember it takes the whole team. Custodians, office staff, cafeteria workers, bus drivers, everyone is part of the team and should support the team values and goals!

## First PD

Do something outside the box to build rapport with your team. Forget the traditional first meeting complete with coffee and bagels. Give them an experience! Take your staff to a ropes course, go bowling, or even take them to an amusement park, where you can all meet up for lunch and a brief introduction meeting! The key here is to build rapport but let your staff that you are willing to go above and beyond to connect with them.

## Remember the Important Events

You can never get another chance to see your daughter's first dance recital or watch your son take his first steps. Yes, it's inevitable that you may have some late nights but that should be the exception, not the norm! It's the same with teachers. I can't tell you the number of times that I got a sub or covered a teacher's class myself so she could watch her own child in a play, or receive a reward in a different grade level or even another school. Teachers never forget when you treat them kindly and ensure they aren't missing out on major life events in their personal lives.

## Ask Questions

I make a rule that about 50 percent of the words coming out of my mouth should end with a question mark in the first 30 days. Part of building rapport is letting your staff know that you value them. Adopting a questioning, coaching style as a leader will also allow others to be more solutions-focused, which in turn empowers them. Questions can encourage a culture of exploration and innovation amongst team members, especially if you model being someone who digs deeper, rather than just accepting the status quo. A team culture that asks questions may also be more willing to risk failing a little more often. A leader who inspires others to take risks and be comfortable with "failure," while at the same time supporting them, will inspire tremendous trust and loyalty.

## Make Them Feel Good about Themselves

If an opportunity arises, pay the person you are talking to a genuine compliment, emphasis on genuine. When we make others feel good about themselves, they naturally warm to us and remember us more positively. In 2004, The Gallup Organization surveyed over four million people globally, and concluded that employees who received regular praise and recognition increased productivity, engaged more with colleagues, and were less likely to leave an organization.

### Value Their Time

Teachers have very little down time. They are always ON. If you want to build good rapport with them, then value their time. Keep their planning time sacred! When teachers are pulled for meetings, committees, or to cover classes, then it takes away from their planning time. This is a rapport killer! Also be mindful about meetings. Here are a few strategies that I used as an administrator to make sure I didn't waste staff time for unproductive meetings because they waste time and zap energy. Make them count by focusing on my six points to better meetings.

* Don't meet if info can be emailed
* Plan an agenda so the meeting is streamlined (30 mins maximum)
* Don't meet just to meet
* Let others lead/share their expertise
* Limit meetings during planning time
* Have coffee/snacks

Finally, when you meet with them individually, respect their time and be attentive. Meet them in their classroom rather than your office, turn off notifications on your phone and computer, and open the conversation by asking questions. Show teachers that you know their time is valuable and that their voices matter.

Building rapport is a science with proven practices and tactics. While these techniques come naturally for some of us, even the most relational person among us can benefit from improvement of our rapport-building skills. Work on any of these techniques and watch your staff rapport soar.

## Becoming the Chief Storyteller

From the beginning of time, we have communicated through stories. Long before there was paper, pencils, or fountain pens, our history, experiences, and lives were shared and passed down through stories. Stories emotionalize information. They give color and depth to data or information and they allow people to connect with the message in a deeper, more meaningful way.

Some of the most successful companies in the world use storytelling very intentionally as a leadership tool. In fact, the corporation giant, Kimberly-Clark, provides two-day seminars to teach its 13-step program for crafting stories and giving presentations with them, and Proctor & Gamble has hired Hollywood movie directors to teach its senior executives how to lead better with storytelling. Even in schools, storytelling should be of high importance. Communicating your story as a leader and your story as a school is important in connecting with your community. After all, you want to control the narrative that your school is speaking to the community. If there is one thing I have learned after 25 years in education, it is that people will tell stories about you and your school whether you want them to or not. Fortunately, you can help choose which ones they tell. The way you do that? You tell them first. You control the narrative. Make sure the stories connect with your audience.

### Building Rapport with Staff

When you first meet your staff, tell a story that's short but something almost anyone could empathize with. Try to make it personal, a bit transparent, and reveal something about you as a human being. Telling a story with which your staff can empathize is a good way to build trust and connect with your staff on a personal, human level.

### Build Rapport with Students

One of the best ways to build rapport with the student body is to share personal stories or experiences in which they can relate as well. I will never forget one of the first assemblies I did with a group of middle school students and I shared my love of video games. This prompted a Friday night video game party where many students showed up to play. I don't think they had ever thought of an administrator as a person before. I let them know that I had played every video game system since Pong was created. I was an OG (original gamer!). On another occasion, I shared with the student body that I was a former bodybuilder and I even had Lee Haney (eight times Mr. Olympia) come to the assembly and speak to the students. What made this occasion special was that many of the fathers came to the assembly, many of whom I had rarely or never seen before. This was a story that they connected with and didn't want to miss!

## Building Rapport with the Parents and Community

Stories have a way of tapping emotions and creating a visceral impact. As I said before, if you don't control the story, other people will. Share the successes in your school. Even if you're new and don't have a narrative yet to share, then share spotlights of your students, teachers, or staff. I shared this idea with a school district several years ago and one of their first spotlights was of their head custodian. The spotlight included that he also played in a band. The custodian was so proud that his story was shared and many students thought it was cool that he was in a band.

Storytelling is an art and a science. But there are a few key elements that are important to effective storytelling. In fact, Paul Smith (2012) author of *Lead with a Story: A Guide to Crafting Business Narratives that Captivate, Convince, and Inspire* says there are seven keys to effective story telling.

1.   *Start with the context.* Ever heard someone excitedly launch into a story and soon the listeners are scratching their heads? The storyteller stops and says something like, "Oh, wait, I guess I should back up a bit and explain why all this happened. You see, my boss had just gotten fired, and so …". That's the sign that the storyteller skipped the context. If they're lucky, the confused look on their audience's faces will remind them to go back and tell the context. If they're not lucky enough to notice, their story is doomed to mediocrity.

2.   *Use metaphors and analogies.* A well-chosen metaphor can add to the impact of a story, or replace a story entirely,

because there are already entire stories attached to those few words in your audience's brain, waiting for you to tap into.

3. *Appeal to emotion*. Studies show people make decisions largely based on emotional reasons, and then rationalize them afterwards so they feel logical. Great leaders know this intuitively, and aren't afraid to lead with both sides of their brain.

4. *Keep it tangible and concrete*. Avoid mind-numbing vague generalities and weasel words typical of management speak today. Keep stories specific and concrete and they'll be more engaging and memorable.

5. *Include a surprise*. Surprises not only get your audience to sit up and pay attention, they make your story more memorable. Studies show surprise triggers the release of adrenaline in the brain that heightens memory formation.

6. *Use a narrative style appropriate for business.* Be concise and to the point. Business narratives should be three to five minutes long. Leave the long soliloquy for your first screenplay.

7. *Move beyond telling your audience a story to creating a scene or event for them to participate in*. While a good story is a close second, experience has always been the best teacher. If you can turn your story into an event that your audience takes part in, it will be even more effective. Don't just tell them about when you found out by accident that your competitor's product worked better than yours. Stage an impromptu situation for them to discover the same thing.

While educators love our data, spread sheets, and test scores, we soon forget them. But we never forget stories. Much like how we don't remember exactly what our favorite teacher taught us, but we remember stories and experiences, and how we felt. This is the power of storytelling. Share the story of your school, of your staff, of your students. Make a strong and lasting connection to your staff, your students, and your community.

## The Pygmalion Effect

This section probably merits a book of its own because it does focus on a part of human nature that can often be overlooked in leadership. I have often said that students will rise to the level of your lowest expectations, but the reality is that this is true of adults as well. I believe that high achievement is usually attained in the context of high expectations.

This was proved to an extent by Rosenthal and Jacobson (1968), who conducted a study of all students in a single California elementary school. They were given a disguised IQ test at the beginning of the study. These scores were not disclosed to teachers. Teachers were told that some of their students (about 20 percent of the school chosen at random) could be expected to be "intellectual bloomers" that year, doing better than expected in comparison to their classmates. The bloomers' names were made known to the teachers. At the end of the study, all students were again tested with the same IQ test used at the beginning of the study. All six grades in both experimental and control groups showed a mean gain in IQ from before the test to after the test. However, First and Second Graders showed statistically significant gains favoring the experimental group of "intellectual bloomers". This led to the conclusion that teacher expectations, particularly for the youngest children, can influence student achievement. Rosenthal and Jacobson (1968) believed that even attitude or mood could positively affect the students when the teacher was made aware of the "bloomers". The teacher may pay closer attention to and even treat the child differently in times of difficulty.

While this first study focused on students, there have been many other studies, which have focused on adults with the same results. In one study, conducted by the Israel Defense Forces, (Eden, 1992) an experiment was conducted on a sample of 105 men with at least 11 years of schooling, who had been selected into a combat command course on the basis of ability and motivation. Their instructors were four experienced training officers. Each instructed a group of about 25 trainees. Trainees were randomly listed as high, average, and low performing.

In the following training it turned out different groups under command of different supervisors showed different results. Trainees of whom high, average, and low performance was expected showed best, average and low results respectively. However, that was not the main surprise of the experiment.

The Pygmalion effect on supervisors rather than subordinates turned out to be even more interesting. Supervisors demonstrated a higher quality leadership towards trainees they thought were the best which in turn promoted better performance. The effect in this case is therefore a leadership phenomenon.

Trainees within the same group reported that they were treated differently by the same supervisors. The ones of whom the best results were expected actually produced them and vice versa. It thus became clear that supervisors could be simultaneously good and bad leaders—it just depended on whom they were leading. Best leadership is thus derived directly from high expectations.

In essence, the **Pygmalion effect** is a type of self-fulfilling prophecy (SFP) in which raising expectations regarding subordinate performance boosts subordinate performance. Managers who are led to expect more of their subordinates lead them to greater achievement.

How is this relevant to you as a principal? How you treat your staff largely determines their job performance. The best leaders create high performance expectations that the staff will fulfill.

As a leader, if you don't think a person can achieve a high level of success then they probably won't. This doesn't necessarily mean that they aren't capable, but that you may not be using your best leadership skills when supervising them because you don't expect them to excel.

The bottom line is this:

* **Leaders,** believe in your team.
* **Hold positive and high expectations** that they will solve that difficult problem, meet the seemingly insurmountable challenges, and more often than not, they will meet or exceed your expectations.

* **Be aware of how you are leading them.** If you don't have high expectations, then you may not be bringing your best leadership skills and thereby you are inhibiting their growth. This also means to expect they can handle any responsibility you give them without micromanaging them or expecting them to do it exactly like you. Give them parameters, ask them to check in if needed, but believe in their ability to succeed. What we think of people, especially when in a position of authority really does become a self-fulfilling prophecy. Make sure theirs is one of success.

## Reducing Burnout

Did you know that we spend over $7 billion dollars a year on teacher attrition and turnover (Carroll, 2007)? Nearly 10 percent of the teaching force leaves the field of education every year. Why is there such turnover? The most common answer from teachers themselves is burnout. They cope with stressful student–teacher ratios, standardized testing, lack of resources, student behavior, ineffective administrations, and more. Teachers feel like they're not making a difference. Teachers are tired.

I have been vocal for a couple of years now about the need to address this vicious cycle of teacher attrition. Imagine if instead of spending $7 billion dollars a year on teacher attrition, we instead spent the money on teacher retention. This means we would focus on the causes of burnout. There are several studies, which cause alarm when we think of teacher health and burnout. But a Gallup study (Wigert & Agrawal, 2018) on burnout revealed five major factors that affect burnout among all employees and which are factors among teachers as well. These five factors were most highly correlated with burnout in the study: So keep these factors in mind and ways to alleviate them as the school year progresses.

1. **Unfair treatment at work**

   When employees strongly agree that they are often treated unfairly at work, they are 2.3 times more likely to experience a high level of burnout. Unfair treatment can include everything from bias, favoritism and mistreatment by a coworker, to unfair compensation or corporate policies. Approximately 25 percent of teachers have said they have felt bullied by their administration. I believe that too often teachers are treated more like students than adults, which means administrators prefer compliance over anything else. Compliance may get some things accomplished in the short term, but it creates a divisive culture and will diminish any rapport you have built with staff. Treat teachers like the professionals they are. I think being seen and treated professionally by administrators is much more important to teachers than how they are perceived by the public.

2. **Unmanageable workload**

   One of the most common responses to burnout among teachers is the workload. Every year we "add to the plate" of teachers, but we never seem to take anything off their plates. Teachers already have too much for us to add just one more thing! At some point that one more thing becomes the straw that broke the camel's back. As the leader, first remove something from their plate before adding anything new. As we have already mentioned, keep their planning time sacred. This could be repeated in every chapter and still not be said enough. Don't use planning time for other duties or meetings. If teachers do not have their planning time, when do you expect them to get it done? At home? Constantly taking planning time will kill morale.

3. **Lack of role clarity**

   Did you know most workers say they don't know what is expected of them at work? When accountability and expectations are moving targets, employees can become exhausted just trying to figure out what people want from them. You may be thinking that a teacher teaches, and that is their role. But there is so much more to the role of a teacher. For instance, how many teachers know exactly what is expected of them going into a school year such as committees, extracurricular activities, teams, and clubs? Even in the classroom, how will they be evaluated, and what are the clearly defined expectations, and job description as a teacher? The best administrators discuss responsibilities and performance goals with their staff and collaborate with them to ensure that expectations are clear and aligned with those goals.

4.  **Lack of communication and support from administration**
    Manager support and frequent communication provide a psychological buffer, so employees know that even if something goes wrong, their manager has their back. Employees who strongly agree that they feel supported by their manager are less likely to experience burnout on a regular basis. In contrast, a negligent or confrontational manager leaves employees feeling uninformed, alone and defensive. Did you know teachers among all professions feel like they are least likely to be heard and their ideas be used by their leaders? Many times teachers may have great ideas to solve problems but are ignored or overlooked. Don't assume because someone is not in a leadership position that they don't have valid views, or that when someone challenges the process that they are against you. Remember the section on handling conflict? It can actually provide solutions.

5.  **Unreasonable time pressure**
    When employees say they often or always have enough time to do all of their work, they are less likely to experience high burnout. Before you create time constraints, remember what it was like to be a teacher. During pre-planning, meetings are important, but remember teachers are probably thinking of all the things they need to do in their classroom. During meetings, if they are not focused or relevant will send teachers into day dreams of working in their room or preparing for the hands on lesson they

have planned for tomorrow. The same is true of minutely detailed lessons plans. I know of a district, which I won't name to protect the guilty, where teachers have to post their detailed plans on their door so administrators can see if they are where they are supposed to be based on the timeline. Is this amount of detail really necessary? Especially when we value differentiation and know plans rarely go as planned. Couldn't this time be better used? Unreasonable expectations, deadlines, and pressure can create a snowball effect, when employees miss one overly aggressive deadline, they fall behind on the next thing they are scheduled to do.

## Burnout Is Not Inevitable

You can prevent and even reverse burnout by changing how you lead your staff. If you don't address the true causes of employee burnout in your school, you won't have a workplace environment that empowers employees to feel and perform their best. Make better use of time and teachers energy. Treat them professionally and make sure you are emphasizing self-care among your staff. When you let your staff know you care about them professionally but also personally, and then make strides to ensure they are taking care of themselves, you create a healthy culture. In fact make one of your PD days all about self-care for your staff. They will appreciate it and you will too!

# Leading with Gratitude

There is an old saying that it is your attitude that determines your altitude. Well there is no better way to create a team full of positive attitudes than with gratitude. However, research (Elton, 2020) suggests that we are least likely to express gratitude in the workplace than anywhere else. Even though, 81 percent of working adults said they would work harder if their boss were more grateful for their work. 96 percent of men and 94 percent of women feel that leaders who express gratitude are more likely to be successful. Gratitude is not only a powerful tool to inspire others, but it is an excellent way to better understand the contributions that others make.

## Steps to Becoming a More Grateful Leader
### *Walk in Their Shoes*

Most administrators were a teacher first. So, for the most part, you have walked in the shoes of a teacher. But it's important to never forget what it was like when you were a teacher. Were you supported, encouraged, and appreciated?

Also, know your staff well enough to empathize with them individually. For instance, you may have a teacher dealing with an elderly parent with health issues, or maybe just had a baby. Walking in their shoes isn't just having shared experiences, but understanding how to help them through their current experiences. They will be grateful to you for being so understanding.

### *Look for Small Wins*

Teachers are always looking for the small wins. Because teachers know that of all things that can boost motivation during a school day, the single most important is making progress in meaningful work. Our job, as leaders, is to express regular gratitude for that incremental progress, and not save our thanks for big wins alone. As I have said elsewhere, small moments build momentum to bigger things.

### *Unexpected*

This one may be a surprise on the list, but think about it. If you get a thank you note from a newlywed couple for the gift you gave, it's rather expected. But if someone surprises you with a thank you, it's a whole different thing. When you get a note from a colleague thanking you, completely unexpected, that can have an incredible impact. One of the ways I gave unexpected praise was to walk into classes for a few minutes, overserve the teacher being amazing and either leave a note for them or email them one shortly after leaving. These little notes may not seem like much, but to teachers they are often seen as small treasures.

## *Share Your Appreciation of Others*

Let people know they matter. This includes communicating this information to staff, students, parents and others. But don't feel you must recognize everyone at once, but take your time and be genuine and specific. It's far more effective than a generic thank you. Let them know for what you're grateful and why it's important to you and other staff members. Sharing gratitude can become a solid strategy for supporting morale and growing motivation.

Gratitude is about recognizing the efforts of your team, but also the individual efforts of those on your team. Leading with gratitude can help create a powerful culture. Gratitude is strongly associated with greater happiness. Gratitude helps people feel emotions that are more positive, enjoy good experiences, improve health, help deal with adversity, and build strong relationships. **In other words, it really helps to rally the troops!**

# 6

# Influencing Culture

**School culture** generally refers to the beliefs, perceptions, relationships, attitudes, and written and unwritten rules that shape and influence every aspect of how a school functions. Students, parents, teachers, administrators, and other staff members all contribute to their school's culture, as do other influences such as the community in which the school is located.

I have often said that I can tell a school's culture within a few minutes of walking into it. How the front office interacts with visitors, how staff interact with each other and students in the hallway. In a positive school culture, there is a positive vibe that is almost palpable and makes you want to be there! The other interesting thing I have noticed over the years is that the schools that best exhibit a positive school culture, spend very little time talking about it and most of the time just doing it. This doesn't mean that they didn't have a process in place, but most schools that spend all their time talking about culture and how to create one, usually do so because they have a very poor culture.

## Shaping Culture

School culture is not the same as the climate of a school. Climate often reflects the relationships among teachers, with families, and with administrators. This doesn't mean the climate is not important, but climate of the school is about mood, it is like the emojis you use to show how you're currently feeling.

Culture, on the other hand, is the values, norms, and patterns of behavior. It's more like the school's personality. It affects every decision, direction, and success of the school. Often those beliefs are so entrenched into the fabric of the school that people don't even think about them when going about their daily routines. This mean that the culture of the school could be negative and hindering success and the staff and students may not even be aware of it. Changing culture is something that doesn't just happen because you talk about culture either, but it takes a focused effort to create a positive and high performing culture. Culture is shaped by several interwoven elements, each of which you as principal do have the power to influence:

1. **Fundamental beliefs and assumptions**, or the things that people at your school consider to be true. For example: All students have the potential to succeed, or teaching is a team sport, or all staff members are valued as professionals and humans. I truly believe that the school family should be seen and cared for just like a family. When this is the foundational belief, everyone knows they supported and valued.

2. **The administrator plans ahead**. Before implementing a new initiative, the leader considers what could present challenges. The leader also consults with staff members that have relevant knowledge to gather as much infor-mation as possible. The leader weighs staff input and is willing to make adjustments if something is not working. It is important to consider views of staff who may dis-agree as well. Remember that your staff is a wealth of knowledge and experience that should be considered a resource not an obstacle.

3. **Shared values**, or the judgments people at your school make about those belief and assumptions—whether they are right or wrong, good or bad, just or unjust. For example: "It's wrong that some of our kindergarteners

may not receive the same opportunity to graduate from a four-year college," or "The right thing is for our teachers to be collaborating with colleagues instead of competing." An important one is to ensure children are learning as children. Such as less focus on high stakes and more focus on learning through play and fun for younger students.

4. **Norms**, or how members believe they *should* act and behave, or what they think is expected of them. For example: First conversation with parents should be a positive one, not one about an incidence. We all should be present and engaged at our weekly grade-level meetings. However, the flipside of this is that you make sure meetings are concise and meaningful as discussed earlier.

5. **Patterns and behaviors**, or the way people *actually* act and behave in your school. For example: There are regularly-scheduled parent engagement nights. Teachers support and collaborate with the teammates. Also, as an administrator make class visits feel like you are there to engage and observe classrooms in actions, not to critique the teacher or class, there is a time and place for formal evaluations. Even greeting staff and students by name in the hall creates healthy behaviors for all to follow. Even allowing staff opportunity to give feedback and input should be a normal pattern of behavior.

6. **Setting the professional tone**. There are three expectations that set the professional tone for your school:

   1) *Be world class*. Whatever your role, be your best self. This is where you as a selfless leader focus on helping everyone reaching their full potential. As I mentioned, you will hire people based upon their strengths, so help them develop those strengths to be world class!

   2) *No surprises*. No assumptions. If something is wrong, I want to hear it from you, not the grapevine. Open two-way communications help create a positive high performing culture. In many schools, the grapevine (informal communication or gossip) often controls what information is shared or exposed. This leads to gotcha moments and it also creates a mistrust among

staff. As a leader, make sure your staff feels comfortable enough to come to you with any problem.

3) *We support each other*. We're a team, not competitors. My motto as an administrator was, "The Best Team Wins!" Too often in education teachers work in isolation and feel like they aren't adequately supported, so competition among teachers and staff will quickly fill that void. Teachers trying to decorate the best room, design the best lesson, etc. just to get attention or feel like they are valued. Make sure your staff always feel supported and you will create a culture where they support each other as well.

Shaping a positive high performing culture is not something done in isolation. It takes team effort and even each of these components influences and drives the others, forming a sphere of reinforcing beliefs and actions. But it begins with you as the leader and the influence you have on the process. Make a plan, involve your staff, treat them like family, and an amazing culture will begin to take shape!

## Implementing Positive Cultural Strategies

As I mentioned above, it is the best team that wins. This is because the whole is greater than the sum of the parts. I have stated many times that "School culture is not created by a mission statement, catch phrases, educational buzzwords or even a set of beliefs, but it is created by the ACTIONS of the whole staff." Implementing a positive culture takes a team effort. But remember, as the leader, you are the thermostat that sets the temperature for the culture to thrive. It begins with the leader and your influence on creating a positive school culture.

Some of the greatest teams in history won consistently because they had a cohesive team. These teams may have had one or two superstars, but they won consistently because of their role players. The coaches knew how to maximize the strengths of the average players. These role players are the average players who perform consistently on a daily basis. They aren't superstars, but they are good and they are dependable. And the coaches know that when they put the right people in the right roles and give them the tools necessary to do their job, success is all but guaranteed. So put the right plan in place, using the talents of your staff and your culture will thrive. Here are a few strategies that I believe will help you create the foundation of an amazing school culture.

## Create a Buzz

I have always liked the term "buzz." When a new product is launched there are advertisement designed to create a buzz. When a new store opens, there is a grand opening with lots of prizes, food, and celebration to create a buzz. I even have a friend who wrote a book called, *What's your Buzz*? He discusses how to create a positive buzz about yourself and your business. As the new leader, or even if you're not new, what can you do to create a buzz about your school? You can do something big, like change the landscaping, paint or draw a mural in the entry way, or it can be something like putting a new electric sign out front. The key is to do something that creates a bit of a buzz among staff, students, and even the community if possible. Coming together around an exciting change or idea helps create a sense of team.

## Unified Vision

While you may have a strong idea of the vision you want for the school, make sure it's not viewed as just your vision. If it is you dictating a vision to your staff, then some will get on board, but some will not. Then you have created division from the start rather than a creating unified vision to bring everyone together. A unified vision is created by seeking input from your whole staff. Everyone from the custodians to your leadership team. The object is to identify the key ideas, values, and beliefs that are the foundation of a powerful vision. One key characteristic of a vision statement is that it is carefully thought-out, clearly articulated, and firmly considers all stakeholders connected to the school. It is about looking forward and seeking to motivate and unify everyone to achieve the very best for the students. The vision needs to capture the aims of a school in its particular context, and guide and inform the preparation of a school development plan. A vision is important for schools, as it:

◆ provides the focus for all aspects of organizational life
◆ informs planning and the development of policies
◆ clarifies and prioritizes the work of individuals
◆ helps to articulate shared beliefs and develop a common language, thereby securing alignment and effective communication
◆ characterizes the organization to the rest of the world

The vision is much more than a few words of vague intention; it embodies the values of the community and is the foundation for actions that will lead to school improvement. By making sure that their vision is clearly focused on a very limited number of clearly articulated and achievable ends. Vision is a high-flying word that has impact only when firmly grounded with what can actually be accomplished in a given time. Vision statements are useless when they are purely aspirational. A period of genuine and constructive listening will provide a you with the information you need to develop a grounded, specific, concise, and clear vision.

## Sense of Priority

The most challenging balancing act a principal faces is fulfilling the managerial and supervisory responsibilities of maintaining a safe, properly functioning school while also serving as an instructional leader and focusing on academic achievement. The best instructional intentions can be diverted by a dreaded call about toilets overflowing or a skunk walking around school grounds. The principal gets called for everything! Although every preparation program stresses the importance of instructional leadership, rarely are enough practical strategies shared for how to do this, and nowhere is there a course on plumbing. Make people, not situations your priority. There will always be important matters or even fires to put out, but if you spend all your time on these, nothing else will get done. You will have to make time for things like visiting classrooms, otherwise, there will never be enough time in the day, and you will won't get around to it. Things like engaging in meaningful discussions with teachers about their practices, and taking every opportunity to lead instruction are ways in which you will ensure a positive culture is developed.

## Small Moments Build Momentum

Often we wait until the end of the year, such as teacher appreciation week, a banquet, or some other "big event" to celebrate successes. Well over time, the small wins will be forgotten and seem unimportant. Recognizing these small wins is as much about being timely as anything else. In the moment, they help keep us inspired and moving forward. It can be hard to build momentum, so start with small wins. The best way to have a successful year is to secure small wins, because small wins often make a huge difference. These small wins make work more meaningful and inspire us to continue forward. So, if a teacher reaches a student who has had issues, for example, celebrate! Affirmation is critical to overall success and even the small wins are wins! Celebrate the small successes because they transform moments into the momentum for great things.

## Start to Design the Agendas for Your First Meetings and Ceremonies

The first meetings, events, and ceremonies you conduct will set the tone for your priorities and your leadership style. Some new principals plan welcoming events before the start of school. These kinds of events help to provide the school community with an opportunity to get to know you. They also go a long way in establishing a sense of community that will be essential. Planning them in advanced will also help you keep them streamlined and on point. You want to share all the information you need to, but you also want to do it in the most efficient and effective manner. Short and sweet will always be a better experience than long and drawn out.

## Trust the Process

Its doing the little things consistent that creates high performing schools. High expectations mean nothing unless you equip people with the what, the why, and the how to execute it. No one is better at this than coach Nick Saban. Even if you're not a big football fan, you have probably heard of Nick Saban, head coach of the University of Alabama football team. He has won more National Championships than any other coach in history. While he is a great coach, he may be an even better leader. When asked about his success he always emphasizes process over everything else. His focus is not on the score of the game, it is on everyone doing their job with excellence. If they make a mistake, they work to correct it and do better next time.

In education we become too product focused. What are our test scores, how did the students do on exams. Yes, outcomes are important, but focusing on the process and how to get better is a growth mindset. Winning the game is important, but Saban knows that it is more likely to happen when all his team trust in the process and work hard to do their best. As the school leader, get your staff to trust the process. Give them the guidance, resources, and opportunities to be their best. When they come up short, help them correct the mistakes and grow from them. Trust the process!

## Organization and Time Management

Trusting the process is in part about effective organization. There is no way you can be an effective principal if you do not have exceptional organization skills. There are so many facets of the job that you can create confusion not only with yourself but with your whole staff. Being unorganized creates chaos and chaos in a school setting especially from a person in a position of leadership can only lead to disaster. Don't expect teachers to be on time if you're often late. When I speak with new principals and mentors, they often share that prioritizing tasks and managing their time effectively can be a major challenge. Be organized, and manage your time effectively. It's also important to help staff members who struggle in this area to do better as well. Even if this means having a PD session to help.

### Create Meaningful Parent/Community Involvement

Generating clear, open communication with the parents of your students can help you avoid misunderstandings and remove feelings of mistrust or resentment. To involve parents in your school culture, give them a platform for feedback on classroom activities or school programs. Involving parents in school activities in a meaningful way also helps foster positive feelings between the school and the parents. You can ask parents to be on event committees or to participate in school fundraisers. I would often ask the PTO, parents, or even businesses to help with activities, like coffee for teachers, or lunch for the staff. This helped create goodwill between the parents, community, and the staff. Teachers loved the appreciation, and the community loved showing their appreciation to the staff.

### Get Feedback and Input from All Stakeholders

While you influence the culture of the school, it's not really a culture if you have the only input into the development of it. Ask yourself, does your staff feel heard, valued, or supported? After 25 years in the educational field, I have come to realize that leaders who truly seek to be their best desire input and feedback from their staff. Those administrators who didn't want feedback seemed defensive about it and usually felt that any kind of feedback was a personal attack. Don't be like this administrator. If you don't want staff to focus on strengths or weaknesses of your leadership, then at the very least ask them what are the things you could do to improve the culture of the school, or that the staff as a whole could do.

Also, don't forget to ask for input from parents and even the community if it affects them. It is best to have a positive and supportive relationship with the community. I remember several years ago when I wanted to add more equipment to our weight room. Rather than having to come up with the resources myself, I reached out to businesses in the community and had the equipment donated because they were sponsors or supported many of our athletic teams.

### Social Media

My brother, who is a sheriff in Georgia, has created a major social media presence for his county. Several months ago, we were discussing that when most people seek the news or hear of an event in the community, they no longer look to the traditional news as they did in the past, but they go on social media, usually local groups on FB related to the county to find out the latest information. Therefore, he decided to create a strong online presence for the Sheriff Department where people in the community could find out the news as quickly as possible. Because they can check out the latest information, he realized that this would increase traffic flow to their site and provide them more opportunities to connect with the community.

♦ **Share updates about your school community.** Social media can be a powerful tool to keep families informed about what's happening in your school. Is there any important assembly coming up for parents? Will tomorrow be a snow day? You can potentially reach thousands of people on Facebook and Twitter.

♦ **Showcase school family achievements for community**. This is a great place to spotlight staff members or even students. It's a no-cost way to showcase activities, team clubs, and sports.

♦ **Create a podcast**. This is a great place for you to create a podcast to share with the school community. You can keep people updated on school events, policy changes, or just have a weekly topic of conversation that helps keep you connected with the parents and community. Invite guests from the community on your podcast to discuss educational issues as they relate to your community.

## Characteristics of a Highly Effective School Culture

A positive school culture is conducive to professional satisfaction, morale, and effectiveness, as well as to student learning, fulfillment, and well-being. The following list is a representative selection of a few characteristics commonly associated with positive school cultures. In fact, this is a handy checklist that you can refer back to from time to time to ensure that you are focused on the right priorities to create a positive school culture.

- There is a clear and shared vision.
- Relationships and interactions are characterized by openness, trust, respect, and appreciation. People are a priority.
- Communication is a two way street. When there is only communication from leadership that one way street quickly becomes a dead end street!
- Staff relationships are collegial, collaborative, and productive, and all staff members are held to high professional standards.
- Students and staff members feel emotionally and physical safe, and the school's policies and facilities promote student safety.
- Mistakes not punished as failures, but they are seen as opportunities to learn and grow for both students and educators.
- Students are consistently held to high academic expectations, and a majority of students meet or exceed those expectations.
- Important leadership decisions are made collaboratively with input from staff members, students, and parents.
- Criticism is constructive and well-intentioned, not antagonistic or self-serving. Conflict can be healthy and lead to growth.
- Educational resources and learning opportunities are equitably distributed, and all students, including minorities and students with disabilities.
- All students have access to the academic support and services they may need to succeed.
- Team is valued over individuals. This creates a culture of collaboration instead of competition.
- Self-care is encouraged and modeled by administration and staff.

♦ Children are allowed to learn as kids. This means adequate recess, unstructured play, and more physical activity/movement in the classrooms.

## Celebrate Teachers

It's interesting that we celebrate musicians, athletes, and Hollywood stars, because we think they're talented, they influence pop culture, and we can relate to them on some level because of their contributions. Ironically, many if not all of them would not be where they are without the encouragement and belief of some teacher. But teachers themselves are rarely given the adulation they deserve when it comes to their talent and influence on others. Teachers are a school's most valuable resource, and after the school leaders influence, there is no one who influences the culture of the school more than the teaching staff. Make sure teachers are appreciated through your words and deeds.

As an educational leader, you have the capacity to build morale by creating a positive work environment. Make teachers feel valued by praising their accomplishments. There are many reasons to celebrate teachers, and here a few key ones:

1. *Everyone wants and needs to be appreciated.*
   Wanting to feel appreciated is a core emotional need for all humans. We all like to feel like what we do matters, that it is appreciated, and that we are appreciated. It's part of our human make-up. A simple verbal thank you, a hand-written note, or a pat on the back can incentivize your teachers to work harder. Celebrating small wins as a team enhances morale; it helps teams maintain focus on what they're working towards while giving everyone a chance to reflect on their successes.
2. *Teachers work so hard.*
   If someone who sings or can score a touchdown is so easily celebrated, then celebrating teachers should be a no brainer. Teachers are some of the hardest workers out there. Anyone who can get up every day to meet the

needs and accommodate learning styles of 30 students per class, deal with parents, prepare lessons, grade tests, all while, inspiring the uninspired, loving the unlovable, and at times, teaching the unteachable deserves to be celebrated every day!

3. *Teachers are difference makers.*

   No other professionals so greatly influence others as teachers do. Just about everyone can point to one or more teachers who have had an impact on their lives. We may not even realize it at the time, but looking back, we can see how certain teachers shaped our thoughts and helped us to achieve far more than we could ever have imagined. They teach us to believe in ourselves and to never say "I can't." Teachers influence the present and the future.

## Call of Duty

As you embark on this journey as a principal or educational leader, remember that it is a privilege to serve the wonderful professionals that are under your command. It will be your influence that will make it an amazing journey or a rough one. Remember it is not just about influence, but positive influence. Anyone can force compliance by the influence of their position, but will this create the best school culture? No, it will not. However, if your influence comes from a place or serving others, to help them be their best, to improve their lives, then you will create the culture you desire. Remember, it's not about your agenda, but about your ability to use your strengths to help others succeed.

As you begin the journey, begin with the end in mind. Don't focus on how successful you will be, what all you will accomplish, but how will my staff and students remember me when I leave. Whether it is one year or 20 years, how will they remember you?

Former U.S. Senator Mark Hatfield tells of touring Calcutta with Mother Teresa. They visited the "Home for the Dying" where sick children are cared for in their last days, and the dispensary where the poor line up by the hundreds to receive medical attention. Watching Mother Teresa minister to these people, and nursing those left by others to die, Hatfield was overwhelmed by the magnitude of the suffering she and her co-workers faced daily. "How can you bear the load without being crushed beneath it?" he asked. Mother Teresa replied, "My dear Senator, I am not called to be successful, I am called to be faithful."

When you lead with a selfless leadership mentality, you won't worry about how successful you are, or how far you climb on the educational ladder, but you will be focused on service. Serving the students, teachers, staff, and the community in which you have been called to lead. Ironically, servant or selfless leaders tend to be the most effective leaders as well as the most enduring leaders to their staff. Not because you are the smartest, wittiest, or even friendliest necessarily, but that you treat them as professionals and as human beings. This is not as common as you might imagine.

Remember, leadership is really a privilege. It is about serving others. So, remember to encourage, support, and show appreciation, and celebrate even the little things. Help your staff and students maximize their potential and help them become their best self. There is no greater legacy than to know your influence made other lives better and more successful.

# References

Abbott, Karen. (2011) The Daredevil of Niagara Falls. *Smithsonian Magazine*, October 18.

Abrashoff, Mike. (2007) *It's Your Ship: Management Techniques from the Best Damn Ship in the Navy*. New York: Grand Central Publishing.

Blasé, Joseph & Blasé, Jo. (1999) Effective Instructional Leadership: Teachers' Perspectives on How Principals Promote Teaching and Learning in Schools. *Sociology*, August.

Booher, Dianna. (2017, December) Personal Interview.

Carroll, Thomas. (2007) *Policy Brief: The High Cost of Teacher Turnover*. Retrieved from http://nctaf.org/wp-content/uploads/2012/01/NCTAF-Cost-of-Teacher-Turnover-2007-policy-brief.pdf

Covey, Steven. (2004) *The 7 Habits of Highly Effective People: Powerful Lessons in Personal Change*. New York: Free Press.

Eden, Dov. (1992) Leadership and Expectations: Pygmalion Effects and Other Self-Fulfilling Prophecies in Organization. *Leadership Quarterly*, 3(4), 271–305.

Elton, Chester. (2020) *Leading with Gratitude: Eight Leadership Practices for Extraordinary Business Results*. New York: Harper Business.

Heathfield, Susan. (2016) The 5 Teams that Every Organization Needs Your Organization's Needs for Teams Will Vary but These Will Get You Started. Retrieved from www.thebalancecareers.com/the-5-teams-that-every-organization-needs-1918507

Iacocca, Lee. (1986) *Iacocca: An Autobiography*. New York: Bantam.

Johnson, Brad & Sessions, Julie. (2016) *From School Administrator to School Leader: 15 Keys to Maximizing Your Leadership Potential*. New York: Routledge.

Kubicek, Jeremie. (2015) *5 Gears: How to Be Present and Productive When There Is Never Enough Time*. New York: Wiley.

Long, Cindy. (2012) Bullying of Teachers Pervasive in Many Schools. *NEA Today*. Retrieved from http://neatoday.org/2012/05/16/bullying-of-teachers-pervasive-in-many-schools-2/

Lopez, Shane J. (2013) U.S. Teachers Love Their Lives, but Struggle in the Workplace. *Gallup News* March 28. Retrieved from https://news.gallup.com/poll/161516/teachers-love-lives-struggleworkplace.aspx

Maxwell, John. (2007) *21 Irrefutable Laws of Leadership.* New York: Thomas Nelson.

NDT Resource. Retrieved from www.nde-ed.org/TeachingResources/ClassroomTips/Teamwork.htm

Oldenburg, Ann. (2016) Bob Hope USO Shows: The One-Man Morale Machine. Retrieved from www.uso.org/stories/154-bob-hope-the-uso-s-one-man-morale-machine

Rosenthal, Robert, & Jacobson, Lenore. (1968) *Pygmalion in the Class-room: Teacher Expectation and Pupils' Intellectual Development.* New York: Holt, Rinehart & Winston.

Ruth, Babe. (2016) Retrieved from www.inc.com/gordontredgold/50-quotes-on-the-importance-and-benets-ofteamwork.html

Seashore Louis, Karen, Leithwood, Kenneth, & Anderson, S. (2010) *Learning from Leadership Project: Investigating the Links to Improved Student Learning.* Minneapolis: Center for Applied Research and Educational Improvement, University of Minnesota.

Shafer, Leah. (2018) What Makes a Good School Culture? Retrieved from www.gse.harvard.edu/news/uk/18/07/what-makes-good-school-culture

Smith, Paul. (2012) *Author of Lead with A Story: A Guide to Crafting Business Narratives that Captivate, Convince, and Inspire.* New York: AMACOM.

Sturt, David & Nordstrom, Todd. (2014) The Evolution of the Manager . . . and What It Means For You. *Forbes*, September 11.

Wigert, Ben & Agrawal, S. (2018) Employee Burnout, Part 1: The 5 Main Causes. *WORKPLACE.* Retrieved from www.gallup.com/work-place/237059/employee-burnout-part-main-causes.aspx

## Other Resources

www.boystowntraining.org/blog_building_supportive_relationships_with_staff.html

www.dialogueworks.com/blog/do-you-communicate-to-control-or-to-connect

www.forbes.com/sites/danschawbel/2012/08/13/how-to-use-
storytelling-as-a-leadership-tool/#1be149e85e8e

www.forbes.com/sites/forbesleadershipforum/2013/04/08/margaret-
thatcher-showed-what-true-leadership-is/#35750bb77f84

https://hbr.org/2017/11/executives-fail-to-execute-strategy-because-
theyre-too-internally-focused

www.hmhco.com/blog/how-and-why-to-use-social-media-as-a-
school-or-district-leader#

www.inscapeconsulting.com/2017/05/effective-leadership-
connecting-vs-communicating/

https://inservice.ascd.org/the-steps-to-creating-a-positive-school-
culture/

https://leadershipfreak.blog/2013/09/30/challenge-the-process-
without-blowing-up/

www.open.edu/openlearncreate/pluginfile.php/135939/mod_
resource/content/4/SL11_AIE_Final.pdf

www.prodigygame.com/blog/school-culture/

www.weareteachers.com/8-ways-build-positive-school-culture-now/